INSIDE

What No One Is Telling the Independent Gospel Artist

DENISE HILL

© 2008
Purpose Press

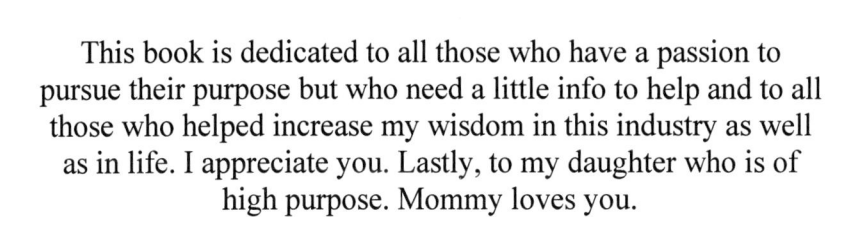

This book is dedicated to all those who have a passion to pursue their purpose but who need a little info to help and to all those who helped increase my wisdom in this industry as well as in life. I appreciate you. Lastly, to my daughter who is of high purpose. Mommy loves you.

"Study to shew thyself approved unto God, a workman that needeth not to be ashamed, rightly dividing the word of truth."
– 2 Timothy 2:15

CONTENTS

FOREWARD

INTRODUCTION

CHAPTER...PAGE

I.   PRODUCT

1. Who are you?...15
2. Is Image Everything?...................................23
3. Do You Hear What I Hear?........................33
4. You Have Our Attention. Now What?.......37

II.   PROMOTIONS

5. You Are the Label......................................43
6. Everything Marketing................................57
7. The Truth About Radio.............................91

III.   PROFITING

8. The Business of It All...............................117
9. You Still Want to Be Signed?..................131

GLOSSARY OF TERMS 143

FOREWARD

Inside-What No One Is Telling the Independent Gospel Artist is a detailed and accurate portrayal of the inner workings of the gospel music industry that few have dared to reveal to up and coming artists. So many young artists look at the glitz and glamour of the music industry and enter into the arena with faulty precepts and misguided intentions. In this tell-all discourse, author Denise Hill does a pristine job in providing readers with the fundamental truths necessary to make informed decisions when it comes to understanding the intricate details of the gospel music industry. In order to be successful it takes an in-depth understanding of how the kingdom of God, musical gifting, and sound business sense mesh together to create a cohesive bond. Passion is the driving force to thrust an individual into his/her purpose; however, many forget that biblical principals have to be the primary foundation.

As a gospel artist for over 25 years I can emphatically say that this discussion is long overdue. Throughout my travels I meet so many young aspiring artists that are trying to find their niche in the gospel music industry. So often they listen to incorrect advice from glory seekers that have prostituted ministry to finance their personal dreams and passions. The knowledge penned in these pages provides the reader with good spiritual and natural advice regarding the perils that lie in the industry. The devil's plan is to take the things of God and use them against the church. Through ignorance and greed many fall prey to his deceptive devices. Finally, the truth is being exposed.

Success in God does not come overnight. Too many artists

are looking for a quick answer. Anything of value in God comes with a price. There are no back doors into the will of God. In this phenomenal book Denise hits these topics of controversy head on. No stone is left unturned. Everyone who reads this book will be equipped with the necessary arsenal to be successful in the gospel music industry. I challenge every reader to take careful notes; the countless resources and personal testimonies, puts this book in a class by itself. Each chapter addresses pertinent and relevant nuggets for reflection and instruction.

This long-awaited blessing to the body of Christ has finally arrived. This book is dedicated to helping all who desire to be great in the gospel music industry. I highly commend Denise for taking on this challenge and I am confident that all who take it to heart will be blessed by this great work. Kudos to you, Denise, for telling **What No One Is Telling the Independent Gospel Artist**.

— Hezekiah Walker

INTRODUCTION

At the time of the initial draft of this book I will be in my 15th year as a professional in the gospel music industry. If you like an additional 10 years can be added to include the years I spent as an artist with one of the nation's largest mass choirs and a local family group. All together that is many years of learning, growing, establishing, developing credibility, building value, and positioning myself to continue to be productive in my career for my family and for the kingdom of God.

Throughout this time my desire has been to work together with like-minded artists, promoters, and labels—filling each others' voids, building on each others' strengths, and working together to achieve the common goal of ministry and prosperity through Christian entertainment. There have been some successes and I have worked with several very talented people. There also have been many setbacks, especially in the early years. I have spent more money than I made, I have been burned by those with agendas and a user spirit, and I have watched the passion of purpose-filled saints be squelched into embers by unmet expectation. Overall, I have learned.

I ate, breathed, and slept marketing, programming, cultural trends, music history, media, and more these many years. The cumulative effect of which has had a direct influence on my success and value in this industry. Moreover, I realize it is all in vain without productivity for the kingdom. I have not learned what I have learned through my many years, relationships, and experiences for me to get glory out of the process.

About seven years into this professional journey I was

connected to an artist and a business situation where I—and what I offered—was clearly the more valuable asset. I was on a top FM radio station in a major market with an audience of 800,000 and was just beginning to build a national audience with XM Satellite Radio. I had a ready-made avenue of promotion, a loyal following, an understanding of what strategies would be most effective for commercial and industry success, and most importantly, I had the passion to press until success was secured. As I designed promo cards and event handbills, hit the streets, worked my show, solicited sponsors, and generally worked my bum off I received nothing but complaints and unrealistic expectations from the artist I worked with. I became the way his or her vision could be realized within his/her limited understanding. I was being used. I do not believe it was malicious, but I do think there was a deliberate belief that this was the way it was supposed to be. He/she is the artist and that should be his/her sole focus; to be an artist. In my efforts to work with others that we may all come up together, unfortunately, I had been in this place before. It always hurt the most when it came from a brother or sister in Christ. There I was again: hurt, frustrated, and questioning why I was again in this position. What was I doing wrong? Who was I supposed to be in this crazy game?

In one of the clearest moments in my life I heard the Father say, "You are a vessel."

Huh? A vessel? You mean I am supposed to be used?

"You are a vessel to be used by me to further my will."

I began to understand that any position I would get in this industry, any connection I would make, any knowledge I would gain would all be for someone else God has been preparing to use. Though I am to use wisdom and not position myself to be maliciously used, the truth was that it was not about me. Holding on to the "how" or some trade secrets serves no purpose and ultimately hinders ministry. If I had not seen this through my work with local holy hip-hop artists or regional up-and-coming gospel artists, it became so clear when, in early 2001, I received a plain silver CD with black lettering from Integrity Records.

There was nothing inspiring about it. There was no fancy imaging or overly ambitious record rep pushing it. It was literally a plain silver sampler with the name "Israel & New Breed" on it that sat on my desk unassumingly for weeks. Had I not been where God placed me with an uncorrupt heart, I never would have played "There's A Lifting of the Hands," and sought Israel out for his first major interview that many would say started it all for the now multi-Grammy winning Israel and New Breed.

Did I discover him? No. God had him on the back side of the mountain before I ever had a radio show. Did I break him? According to the industry, yes, but to me, no. I was a vessel used by God in this particular industry to further His purpose for that particular artist and ministry and it was my privilege. It is with that same heart I desire to share vital information with you.

Many times independent artists, indies, unsigned artists, or whichever title works for you, travel the route of most resistance because they simply do not know. No one told them it is counter-productive to have your entire family call a radio station and request your song. They do not understand how important a visual presentation is. Many indies think the platinum-selling artist is the most important person in the entourage, not knowing it's, in fact, the person next to them. Most have no clue that spending 80% of your budget in the studio will almost certainly guarantee you a house full of unsold product. There are common misconceptions and lack of knowledge that are just difficult to counter or fully overcome at any workshop, conference, or seminar and the enemy uses these challenges to discourage ministries into forfeiting the position in the kingdom and the Earth that God has called you.

Use me! As a vessel, I have attempted to stuff as much information as I can into this book addressing the three main areas where independent artists fall short. A signed artist has a team of folks who have already figured these things out and can implement them successfully for them. In addition to their team they have colleagues in the industry who have gone before them and can show them the way. You are your team. You are your label. With this book you have someone that has gone before you who knows the way. You are now better equipped to go forth and succeed.

This book may not be complete in the eyes of many. There perhaps are some areas of disagreement with many of my contemporaries as well. I do not proclaim this as "The Independent Artist's Bible." Just take what you need and what will help you. As my Bishop would say, eat the meat and spit out the bones, and the realization of your professional music ministry goals according to His purpose will be revealed.

—Denise R. Hill

Part I

PRODUCT

Chapter 1

WHO ARE YOU?

Who are you? I know that is a loaded question but in this industry, it is a question in which the simplest answer is the best. You see, who you are will determine how you apply everything else we will discuss in this book. Please understand the question is not solely professional, but personal as well.

Personally, who are you? Are you a person of integrity? Is this a side hustle or a full-time career endeavor? Are you a person of sacrifice or selfishness? Are you egotistical or humble? Are you a person of vision or conservative in thought? Why do I ask? A person of limited integrity, untrustworthy out of the public eye, will likely compromise the kingdom for monetary gain. Do not forget that when you are a "gospel" or "Christian" artist, you represent something other than yourself.

I have heard artists like Tonéx and Yolanda Adams say, "I am an entertainer." That is true but I further believe that once you build your career upon the foundation of gospel and proclaim Christ is who you serve then now you are a gospel entertainer. You represent the kingdom of God. You can not behave the same as a secular artist simply because you have acquired the financial success or popularity familiar in the secular community. Can you hold to who you are in Christ?

Pastors who call for $100 offering lines and drive Bentleys while their parishioners are on the bus are few in number. However, the few have created a perception of the whole, damaging the perception of the body. Will you? Are you a person of integrity?

Is this a side hustle for you or a full-time career goal? The principle of reaping and sowing is very real in this industry. You will get out what you put in. A person who perhaps enjoys singing or rapping but sees this as a hobby or part-time work will get those same results. You will not be available to connect with the ones who may be in a position to further your efforts because your focus will be toward another area of your life. The ministry and performance opportunities that are already few and far between for independent artists will continue to elude you, as your time and energy are not dedicated to this task. Many are surprised upon meeting me as to how young I am. I made it to the number one market in the world, New York City, to program the number one gospel station in the nation by age 35. Though I trust God's timing, because of distractions and lack of commitment I also understand the opportunities I missed to shave some years off that time. Is this your side hustle or a full-time career endeavor?

Are you a person of sacrifice or selfishness? To make it professionally in this industry you must be willing to sacrifice much. Often times sleep is elusive. There are late hours working on the vision so not to upset the balance with family, for example. What about that latte each morning? Do you have to have it, or is that money that can be saved for the promotional campaign bill you will need to foot as an independent artist? And what about the non-tangible things associated with your success? Do you share information about engagements or opportunities with other aspiring artists or horde them for what you believe is your benefit? Had I chosen to take the wisdom of my experiences and keep them for myself, you, the reader would not have access to the vital information in this book, but there also would be no pouring out for me to make room for the Father to refill with a fresh anointing, fresh Word, new vision, and new experiences. Who are you, a person of sacrifice or selfishness?

Are you egotistical or humble? Can someone talk to you and tell you how your ministry has blessed them without you taking the glory for yourself, or will you expect that your ministry is blessing and look forward to the accolades? Having nasty attitudes, diva-like behavior, and being unapproachable are liabilities to a professional music career and are issues similar to the one of integrity discussed earlier. I will never forget some years ago when a popular gospel duo stopped by the radio station to promote their new project. I conducted the interview as arranged and while the "On Air" light was on, the warm Christian character was front and center. When their purpose was fulfilled and the interview was over one of the duo could not be bothered longer with any polite banter or casual conversation. The attitude was so unwelcoming that I could not publicly support their music ministry any longer. The music is played but I do not volunteer my support as I would to an artist who makes an effort to exemplify the Christ they sing about.

That example is something that is easily protected within the walls of the body but what about the world? Recently an unsaved co-worker of mine came to me and was so distraught at the attitude of one of our female platinum-selling gospel artists. He barged through the studio door yelling, "Church folk, church folk. I can't stand church folk." The good news was that he did not consider me "church folk," and that I was in a position to encourage him to focus back on the Father and not the person. The bad news was that an eye roll and no passing "Good morning" in the hallway reinforced his negative perception of the body of Christ. Which person are you? Are you one who will reinforce negative perceptions or will you be the standard?

Are you a person of vision or conservative in thought? This is an industry where the more you see without seeing, the further you will progress. If you can see the bend in the road before it reaches you, God can position you to endure. Musically and business wise, many independent artists find themselves playing catch up. Their music is dated according to the current trends, yet they have stubbornly convinced themselves they are the next big thing bringing something new to the game. With their image and presentation unfocused, they tell media, "I got something for everybody," rather than sensing the next move of God and the industry or seeing the market void and presenting that. Vision paired with risk-taking, instead of conservative "I'm-only-going-to-go-this-far" thinking is key to success beyond your local church. You must consider who you are.

Once the personal questions are answered you must address the professional ones. Remember, you are the label. You represent you. It is your vision according to His purpose. The "you" you believe you are professionally will serve as the barometer for effectiveness and productivity in each circumstance that may present itself to your ministry. In other words, you will know whether you are progressing in the right direction or wasting time by revisiting the standard you have set for who you are as an artist.

The name "Dark Child" brings to mind club jams with crazy beats. Mention Kurt Carr, and the song every praise team will sing becomes the central thought. Kirk Franklin will help you get your praise on. The Canton Spirituals will hit a hard-driving song for 25 minutes straight. That is just who these artists are. Are they capable of successfully offering other expressions to their artistic body of work? Absolutely, and they sometimes do, but what you need to understand about them (and yourself) is that there is a space, perfectly shaped and designed by God to accomplish His goals in reaching who they (and you) are assigned to reach.

Kirk Franklin has written "Why We Sing" and "Imagine Me." These are two of the greatest worship songs in contemporary gospel music history, ushering individuals into an up-close and intimate place with the Father. He is well capable of tapping into many emotions and aspects of our spiritual walk. But if we were to solely have that portion of Kirk Franklin without the praise party, bridging-the-gap jams that the world embraces as well as the church, would he be as effective? Would he be as popular? Would he be the multi-platinum selling artist he is today? I submit to you he would not.

God will use what He chooses but He has a perfect will as well, and that is that spot that only you can fill to address an issue, area, or a specific part of the body that is your audience. Who are you? Are you the praise and worship leader? Are you the holy hip-hop head? Are you the hard driver? Are you the inspirational artist or the church musician? Who are you?

The answer to this question is the culmination of the answers to three questions all should ask when entering a public ministry. They are:

What am I saying?
To whom am I saying it?
How am I saying it?

These questions can quickly be answered in the flesh by the person who has some of the personal challenges discussed earlier in this chapter. However, I encourage you to take this to the Father for His response. If you do that upfront it will save you much time and energy, enabling you to head in the exact direction He would have you go – toward that spot perfectly designed for you. The more your flesh and your desires get involved in this process, the greater the risk of being off-track and in dangerous spiritually uncovered territory.

As a radio personality it has always bothered me to hear an artist say, "I got something for everybody. There is some hip-hop for the young folks, some church for grandma, and just good music for everyone else." What? So you are just all over the place, huh? Lack of focus and direction is a guaranteed way to shorten your presence in this industry. As I reflect back in my mind, each of the artists that I recall having something for everyone now has nothing for anyone. They are no longer productive contributors to the Christian entertainment industry. They have not released a CD in years. A sold-out dedication to a specific vision is a must.

Again, God may use you in other areas and for other purposes. Though your niche is quartet he may have you do a duet with a rapper. He reserves that right but those opportunities should never be viewed as an addendum to His initial plan for you. He does not change. Jesus could have stayed and had a long and prosperous ministry healing and performing miracles, but He had a place He needed to go. The initial plan of God for Jesus to be the perfect sacrifice never changed though he was used in other capacities. The same holds true for your music ministry. Who are you?

Marvin Sapp has been an artist for many years. From his days with Commissioned to his very successful solo career he has been consistent in his purpose and place in the industry and kingdom. No matter how many times I interview him and ask him about his music, his answer through the years has remained unchanged. "My music is to encourage the body of Christ. It's for the saints," he says. "Whosoever Will," "Grace and Mercy," and "I Believe" are all songs whose message has been to encourage the body of Christ through various circumstances and situations. Though "Never Would Have Made It" found great commercial success and recognition from the secular community as a great inspiration, Marvin Sapp has remained true to the purpose and focus of his ministry. What he says is encouraging, it is to the body of Christ, and he does it through song and preaching. He has discovered the culminating answer to the questions "What are you saying," "Who are you saying it to," and "How are you saying it?" and has let that lead his professional and ministry choices. You absolutely must do the same.

A fourth question I would like you to consider is, what is your goal? Do you want to make money or be famous? You will not do both, especially in your early years. As an independent artist the process and resources needed to be known nationwide or worldwide will likely not be at your disposal. Those are readily available to labels, however, which will serve as a continual challenge to your decision to be an independent artist, as opposed to a signed and contracted label artist. The con is lack of popularity but the pro is that for every $15 CD you sell you get to keep $15. A signed artist is doing good to get $0.20 for each CD sold (more in chapter 9).

In discovering and walking in who you are you must be comfortable with your decision to be an independent artist and all that comes or does not come with that. Know that as your success as an independent artist begins to grow the two roads will meet. I am not just referring to the roads of fame and financial prosperity but also the roads of purpose and divine timing. Do not get distracted. Whether it is character, talent, ministry, or value know every level of who you are in this industry and in the kingdom. Trust me: who you say you are will be tested and tempted, and if you waiver you fall into the trap of being told by the industry and consumers who you are to be for them. Do not be satisfied with just knowing who you are, but develop an unshakable understanding of yourself and your purpose.

Chapter 2

IS IMAGE EVERYTHING?

The simplest answer is yes. Of course with Christ as our Lord and Savior we know there is more, including anointing, divine timing, etc. But the industry answer is "yes," image is everything. A more accurate way to say it is "perception is everything" and the question does not relate just to your promotional photos or stage presence as many independent artists think. There are so many more questions relating to your image.

How does the audience perceive you? How do radio and the media see you? How do promoters perceive you? Are you perceived as an artist for the youth? Are you perceived as a traditional artist? Do promoters see you as a "difficult to deal with" artist? Does radio see you as a core artist? Does the audience perceive you as anointed and energetic or too worldly? The answers to these questions and more are what make up your image, how you are viewed, and ultimately how the industry will deal with you.

AUDIENCE

People tend to use the arts as an extension of their personalities. It is a reflection of what is in them and who they are. Rarely will you find someone who has their jeans sagging and their baseball cap pulled down over their eyes enjoying Bach as their primary music choice. There are eclectic individuals that like a variety of music but everyone has a primary genre of music they prefer and their lifestyles reflect. The same holds true within the body of Christ.

That same brother with the baggy jeans and baseball cap who is saved will likely enjoy the urban or hip-hop music of the kingdom. The natural woman who enjoys poetry, journaling, and the soulful things of life will likely enjoy gospel neo-soul, jazz, and contemporary gospel. The point to these examples is to stress how important it is reflect your audience as much as possible. Or better still find the audience that best reflects you. This will be the foundation upon which your future success will be built.

The mainstream mindset is that anyone is a potential consumer of your product. That is true but for an independent artist who has to recoup monies they invest in themselves as well as establish themselves as a professional artist, it becomes crucial to focus on the audience that will support you because they identify with you. It is better to establish a core audience that will return to you as long as they can see you in them and them in you.

There are artists that are manufactured by labels to mimic the image of the popular culture. More times than not those artists go down in history as a flash in the industry pan or as a one hit wonder. The cultural trends change and the next flavor of the month is up. The record label and industry milked that artist until their shelf life was up, took the money, and moved on to present the next flavor the culture would accept. Do not let that be you.

If you have established a particular style of dress, sound of music, form of speech, etc., rather than change that to be the next Kirk Franklin, Fred Hammond, or Israel, be who you are with any needed professional touches to make you the best you. Then present that image. If you are manufactured the audience will find you out. Pretending you are quartet, for example, to have access to the continual flow of quartet concerts is fraud. You have to have that in your heart for it to truly manifest in your image, performance, and music. If you are exposed as a fraud or opportunist it could mar your name in your city and in the industry. Please be mindful, though this is a great big world it is truly a small one as well. Everyone talks and when something negative is passed about someone, it is remembered – and future decisions are made on that information all without meeting the person. Do not let that be you.

Represent the image of your core audience. The trends of popular culture have a beginning and end to their seasons. Your image will represent the mainstream in God's time and as seasons change. When that time presents itself, be ready – having tried what works, made your adjustments, and settled with that audience you established in your formative years as an artist.

Furthermore, just like the industry have standards, so do audiences. They may not look at you with the same eye as a program director or promoter but they are critical nonetheless. Even when the grungiest rock artist hits the stage or attends a photo shoot for promotional materials or an album cover, he/she is still professionally put together. Every rip in the leg of jeans is frayed just right, each renegade strand of hair is positioned and sprayed into place, each baggy button-up or flannel has been chosen to perfectly complement skin tone. Nothing has been grabbed from the floor and just thrown on as the impression would give, but rather each element is professionally orchestrated to achieve a particular look or image that, while identifiable to the audience, is presented on a higher level.

Audiences like their superstars. Most audiences, even gospel, utilize entertainment as an escape from the everyday. Though the music and artist should reflect their audience, you as the artist cannot be your audience. There has to be a separation, or the appearance of a separation, in quality through your image and what you present as an artist, giving your audience something to identify with – yet still seek to attain. Any audience is savvy enough to distinguish between an amateur (someone who is unrefined and inexperienced) and a professional (someone who is skilled at their craft). Being an independent artist does not mean you are or should present yourself as an amateur. Being signed is not the mark of a professional. Delivering the goods and actually being professional is the mark of a professional.

You want an audience to buy your product, purchase your concert tickets, and collect your merchandise then they must perceive that you are worth it. As I began to grow in this industry I had to practice this myself. I am the jeans, t-shirt, and ponytail girl to the core. I would dress it up when I had to be on stage but would do the jeans, t-shirt, and ponytail any other time. During my time in D.C. I got glimpses of a need for me to do better. One particular time I was in the mall with my family, just hanging out and playing around with my then toddler daughter. Little did I know there was a minister nearby who recognized me.

Perhaps because it was the weekend and I was with my daughter he excused my completely disheveled appearance but a part of me was embarrassed. That same feeling repeated itself one instance when I bumped into a fan while coming out of the grocery store, and another when I was recognized at a friend's recording. If I was going to be "The Gospel Lady," I needed to learn how to present myself the way I was perceived. If jeans were my thing then I needed the best, crispest jeans. If t-shirts were my thing, I would need to transition from baggy men's tees to fitted fashion tees and match them up with some wedges and dangling earrings. My budget and know-how were limited, so I began to buy a few quality pieces to mix and match here and there. I began to build my image for every situation: casual, stage, leisure, etc. Yes, your presentation is continual when you are a public figure as a successful artist is.

Make sure you pay attention to the image you present your audience. Hire an image consultant or personal shopper. Get books on fashion and how to apply make-up. Make the effort to present your audience with your best. If you never get commercial radio airplay this audience will be the foundation of your music ministry.

MEDIA

Mary Mary found much success right out of the gate in 2000 with their first hit, "Shackles." The foundation of that success was built on a mainstream audience. They were on a secular label and were treated with the same marketing blueprint laid out for your average R&B artist. Video, Urban (FM) airplay, appearances on the mainstream television shows – first year, gospel media was an afterthought to the industry and label professionals who were creating their image and directing their career. With a platinum hit in mainstream media, having Mary Mary visit an AM gospel radio station for an interview or make a promotional appearance at a gospel station's event did not compare to a 30,000 seat stadium event alongside the top secular artists.

Please know, what the professionals of a label choose to do with a signed artists may or may not be the actual desire of the artists so I am not saying one over the other was the choice of the ladies of Mary Mary. But the reality is that they were established as mainstream artists rather than gospel artists. This frustrated many in the gospel media community.

At this time I was on my grind in the industry. I lived what I continue to preach to others: I was eating, breathing, and sleeping my profession. Not yet a program director, I was a program assistant, a personality on 2 stations in Washington, D.C. plus one on XM satellite radio. That and regular conference calls with other personalities and program directors across the nation afforded me the opportunity to experience how the perception of radio could affect the support of a project and artist. The Mary Mary scenario is one of many that is burned into my professional memory.

The extent of the gospel media's frustration did not show its face until the follow-up Mary Mary project was released. One would assume any personality or program director would want to get a hold of music from a platinum-selling gospel artist for their radio station. Not so. The instant whirlwind mainstream success of their debut release was not to be mimicked with their sophomore project. The project struggled to connect with that same secular audience. In the meantime a marketing campaign was launched for Christian and gospel media. The secular label enlisted the services of a gospel radio promoter with relationships in gospel radio to achieve airplay and exposure. Needless to say, this left folks feeling like second fiddle. The same was not done for their debut release. The bitter comments I heard within gospel radio were, "Now they want an interview ...," and "We couldn't get a call when 'Shackles' was out." One programmer, when faced with an interview opportunity told me, "I have nothing to ask them." I must admit I understood the frustration and experienced some myself. It is never good feeling like you are being used, and though that is the nature of this business, this particular situation was so overt.

Erika and Tina, the ladies of Mary Mary, may not know to this day that they lost the respect and support of many gospel announcers and program directors and were perceived as opportunists. The point is this: it matters how the media professionals you will need to promote and market your project perceive you. It will determine to what degree they support and push you.

In another respect, how these same industry professionals perceive you based on your CD cover, marketing material, etc., will also affect their interest and future support of you. If you look like a quartet and a station's playlist is primarily contemporary gospel a program director will be in no hurry to review your music, much less add it to their rotation.

As the host of a gospel show on a secular station I was responsible for programming Sunday mornings. As such I had a designated music day as most program directors do. One day an independent label rep met me to pitch his all-girl group. He described them as having a contemporary sound like Kirk Franklin with praise party beats and great vocals. That type of artist was perfect for my programming. After all, my demo was 18-34 focusing on urban inspiration and contemporary gospel music. I had to check this group out. When the rep handed me the CD and pulled out his poster I looked and saw 5 ladies with highly spritzed pin-ups and hard curls, lime green dress suits with matching lime green heels set in front of a colorful psychedelic background.

"Who is this?" I asked. No way was this a Kirk Franklin type girls group. They surely must be the next be thing in quartets. The label rep reassured me and requested I listen to their CD. The music was a gospel techno house blend. Here I was being presented with a description of an urban inspirational artist who looked like a traditional quartet but sounded like CeCe Peniston. I never played that group. Their only potential for airplay came in that sole visit by their label rep. Had that CD landed on my desk from the mail it would have immediately been dismissed without review simply because it appeared to not fit the vision of the programming.

Please take and apply the point that how your character, visual representation, and you as an artist are perceived will affect your relationship with gospel and Christian media industry professionals subsequently affecting your exposure and promotional support.

PROMOTERS

Money, money, money, money – that is what promoters are about. Yes many are also about offering quality Christian entertainment the entire family can enjoy and that edifies the body. But believe me, if a promoter does not make a profit or at least break even from the expenses associated with offering that good Christian entertainment, they will not remain promoters for long. It is about making money. Even the basic church revival takes an offering. There are costs incurred every time the doors open and lights are turned on. Will your image and name bring in money? Many promoters will insist it is about bringing in people but logically speaking, people are money.

Your image and name has value. Whether the value is small compared to a platinum artist is irrelevant. It has a value attached to it. Your image may affect how a promoter believes they can benefit from your value. You see, if a promoter hypothetically is working to put together a tour called "The Praise and Worship Tour," and you and your music ministry are steeped in youth and holy hip hop, chances are that promoter will not see you as a fit. That by no means implies you should change your image to fit an opportunity. The very first chapter of this book was about knowing who you are so no opportunity, amount of money, consultant or such can change the direction God has you going. The only thing you need to understand from this is that your image may exclude you from fitting in someone else's vision for their event. Likewise, it may include you in many as well.

While on the topic of your image and promoters, I may as well expose the unfortunate side of this business. Remember when you are talking about event promoters you are talking money and position in the industry. I have known independent artists that have or were attempted to sabotage performance and ministry opportunities of other artists who have a similar image and draw as they do. It is not unheard of to have an artist contact a promoter after they have begun conversations with another artist or even already booked them. The offending artist will begin their sales pitch and promise the world. "I will put you on my web site." "I have a street team that will hand out your flyers." "You won't need to pay me, just give me a table to sell my product." These and more have been spoken by many an independent artist (and some national artists) in an effort to convince a promoter to book them instead of or in addition to another artist.

Do not fall into the flesh trap of needing to protect your image or compete to establish yourself. The wrong motivation is in your heart at that point. Contacting promoters is a basic business practice of artists and their representatives in the industry. But when it is done to better your ministry over another or to compete you enter dangerous territory. Have you ever heard "touch not my anointed?" Not saying your ministry is not anointed, but the ministry you are seeking to one up may be favored and in right standing concerning their ministry and their personal walk. Do not think because your lyrics are concerning the Father that you are exempt from His disciplining hand. It is not worth it. Do you and let the Father do the rest.

Chapter 3

DO YOU HEAR WHAT I HEAR?

Much like there are different perceptions of your image based on the needs of the individual perceiving you, people hear and listen differently depending on who they are and their needs. Unfortunately many independent artists, especially those just beginning their journey, are listening to their music with their heart. They do not take the time to listen from an audience's perspective or a radio perspective for example. It is primarily about what they like and not necessarily about what is needed for success in the industry or reflective of the current trends in music.

This is one major reason why holy hip-hop or gospel rap, if you prefer – has not found an audience in gospel radio. Most gospel rappers get in the studio, get to making beats, then they press record and start flowing. There is little thought behind the track other than what the individual or their immediate circle says is hot. Well, that does not work for everyone else because the masses do not subscribe to holy hip-hop as their primary music choice. Truthfully, the African American church, gospel's primary audience does not have holy hip hop as their primary music choice. It is more prevalent and profitable in the Christian market. However most holy hip hop artists are more comfortable with an audience that looks like them or their church where they have minister so that point is mute. In my experience, that advice has far too often fallen on deaf ears.

If the average holy hip hop artist listened throughout their production process, considering the needs of industry aspects rather than solely the narrow focus of their tracks and rhymes, they would find more success within the gospel music industry. If you reflect on artists that have found overall success of this particular form of gospel, you will notice they have a track listing that appeases their audience, encompasses what radio is seeking, and has what is needed for the stage or video. More specifically, there are songs that the core audience will bounce to in their car, a selection or two that is not intrusive and blend well with the overall programming of a radio station, and tracks that work well to capture and keep an audiences attention while performing on stage, television, or DVD. Of course there will always be what the industry calls "album tracks." Those are songs that are good songs that the listener will appreciate but are likely not hits for radio or performance jams.

The problem comes when artists try to find industry success with all album tracks. That rarely works. The audience loves it but radio rejects it then the artist becomes frustrated as they compare the quality of their presentation to another artist getting airplay. I can not tell you how many consultations I have had with artists and how many meetings during tracking times I have had where the artists or label rep gets completely worked-up that they are getting no play. There are numerous influences that I speak more on this in chapter 7 of this book concerning radio. But for the purpose of this chapter you must understand what you do for your artistic fulfillment is not necessarily what radio needs for its programming purposes. It is not.

You love gospel rap. Your primary audience loves gospel rap. They always will. When you submit something to radio as a part of your promotional campaign or to a promoter for consideration, guess what: they are not just considering your gospel rap audience. There is a greater portion of the population who want their needs satisfied and who are willing to pay money for it. The same holds true for quartet, neo-soul, gospel jazz – anything non-mainstream. Through your music you must find a way to present something that will be useful to all.

When I present this scenario to many artists they feel almost offended, as though I am asking them to water down their music. As an artist I understand that perspective. That is why it is so important to know what you want. What is your goal? If any part of it has to do with reaching the masses through media then you need to understand you may have to make compromises to deliver on those media needs. If you are the quality, anointed, and inspired artist or producer you claim to be, you will find a way to offer the industry something useful that you are pleased with. The general sentiment among gospel program directors is, "just give me something to play." There is not a conspiracy to keep everyone except Kirk Franklin off the radio. Just give programmers something to meet their programming goals that they can play without jeopardizing the station's core audience. Radio and Christian media must to be able to perceive you as an asset to their programming. Not a liability.

Chapter 4

<u>YOU HAVE OUR ATTENTION. NOW WHAT?</u>

Many of you who are parents can easily visualize the following scenario. You and your adult family or friends are gathered together enjoying conversation, laughter, and probably some food. Perhaps you are in your home and at a family gathering. Adults are working and focused on responsibility and taking care of the family and household that when you get multiple folks together it is good fellowship and fun. As you converse louder and louder as adults do, all of a sudden there is a child standing in the midst staring up at you. Of course you know you told the kids to go play but that innocent face looking up will not let you fuss. As you stop mid-sentence others nearby notice the distraction as well and want to see what is wrong. Who hit who? Is someone hurt? Do I need to go upstairs? These and more are the typical questions answered without asking when the child first runs up the stairs from the basement but not this time. They just stand there looking, prompting you to ask, "How may I help you?"

All eyes are on the child as parents anxiously wait to see if its child that is the offender or injured. With a slouch and a lean in to sit on your lap the child calmly says, "Nothing I just wanted to sit with you." That is the buildup and letdown of many independent artists both on stage and on CD. You have a captive audience. They are either voluntarily sitting in an audience or willingly spent their money on your project or download and the expectations were not met.

Far too often have I been hired to host a concert or event and left with a purse full of CDs from aspiring artists seeking airplay on my show. With many I was excited to get their project. There were times I was so moved by their performance that I purchased one myself to support their ministry. For a radio person to buy a CD rather than ask to be serviced one for free is a big thing. I inserted the CD in my player and went directly to the song I knew would be a hit. After all I just heard it and went straight into praise or worship. This is going to be great. Not. The song that was ministered on stage did not translate into a hit on the CD. In many cases it was not even a good song. The production quality was poor, the vocals were not tight, and the free flowing spirit and anointing on the performance I saw was not the same on the CD I listened to. But when I was approached I was given the impression this was fire! It was the hottest thing to hit gospel music. After one concert I was told by an artist, "If you liked that you will love this." After listening to the project I had to wonder, 'What are you hearing that I am not?' There was nothing I could use on the radio.

When you get the attention of someone, especially anyone in the industry, you must have the complete goods to deliver. You can not just be great on stage, you must have a project that displays who you are, an image that reflects your music, and more.

The flip side of that is you can not just have a great CD. When the lovers of your ministry come to see you, especially if they have paid to see you, there must be success in meeting their expectations. The word of fabulous concerts and tours spread quickly among consumers. They tell others, "You have got to see them in concert," or "They turned it out." News of your wonderfulness live will not only travel but it will stay in the memory of the audience increasing your value as an artist to promoters for future opportunities.

Likewise, poor performances and presentations will spread quickly and too affect your value. If you do not have them on their feet during the concert and talking about you after the concert you will likely be viewed as an artist that is not worth the ticket price, nor worth including on future concerts over another artist that has and will deliver powerful performances.

Once a contract is signed with a promoter and you are promised to minister, that promoter becomes captive to your abilities. Likewise, once an audience has purchased tickets, entered an auditorium or church, and claimed their seat, they become a captive audience. You asked for the attention, make sure you give everyone the understanding that you and your music is worth it. You can claim the attention easily, but you must work to earn the respect.

I am well aware many of you reading this book may be at the very beginning of your journey and a few years from this place of professionalism. That is okay. Use this when considering your presentation as you move forth so you do not make some of the same mistakes others have before you. Make sure you offer something whether on stage, in person, or on a disc that will benefit you and do not offer something that will be a liability to your career as an artist. Many of the artists who disappointed after the build up did not get a second chance to impress. Future projects were dismissed and they remain "local artists." Do not let that be you.

Part II

PROMOTIONS

Chapter 5

<u>YOU ARE THE LABEL</u>

When God gave you the vision to sing or rap or play your instrument in a public ministry with you positioning yourself as the artist, He gave that vision to you. It was likely an intimate moment between just you and Him, and that is exactly how you as an independent artist will go forth: just you and Him. According to thefreedictionary.com the very definition of the word independent is "self-governing or self-reliant." That means your industry success or failure depends totally on you.

That is a lot of pressure when you look at it that way. Everything from the beginning when you made the decision to be an artist, to the end when you attain a measure of success, is a burden set squarely and completely on your shoulders. You are responsible for finding and securing an adequate studio, finding a producer or developing tracks, writing lyrics, mastering and duplication, graphic design for CD and promotional materials, organizing photo shoots, negotiating distribution and establishing consignment deals, promotion and marketing, radio servicing and tracking, publicity, arranging tours, etc., etc., etc.; they are all your responsibility and, most importantly, are at your expense.

There is no second party to foot the bill, to develop or execute the vision, nor – in times of naiveté – to advise or secure an expert's counsel. All the funds you have are your savings, your paycheck, or your churches funds. You are not just undertaking a ministry but also a business venture. As in any business venture, goals and objectives must be set to gauge your level of success. Your label is no exception. If any monetary, professional, and personal investment is made toward a recording project or artist, an equal or greater outcome should be expected and achieved. Unaware of current industry practices or consumer trends, many artists make the mistake of expecting unrealistic financial and business outcomes.

Because the investment is so personal it often appears greater than it truly is compared to others within the industry. The $2500 that came directly from your paycheck for the duplication of 1,000 CDs likely put a dent in your household finances. However, it would be unrealistic to expect to reap within a year the financial return of a platinum selling artist off a $2,500 investment.

Furthermore, because an indie artist has control of his/her own success, I have met many artists filled with visions of grandeur, popularity, and financial success rather than focusing on the ministry of the music with a business mind. This diverted focus contaminates the works and makes it difficult for the ministry to prosper. As the saying goes, "you block your own blessing." Realistic results must be evaluated from a spiritual as well as business perspective. For a little more detail there are a few things we should discuss: balance, strategy, and humility.

BALANCE

While the cost of becoming a commercial recording artist is your financial burden to bear, so are the finances and maintenance of your household. I have worked with many independent artists. The bulk of them have been not just men but men, with wives and children. I cannot explain to you the heart-breaking pain I have felt seeing them struggle with the challenge of continuing their ministry and artistic dreams while striving to be the successful head of the household God called them to be. Needless to say the pain was not limited to me.

There was plenty to go around. I have seen wives hurting from the reality of mounting bills and household necessities while fighting to stay supportive of their husband's ministry and goals. I have seen children suffer from the lack of parental attention while dad is off to grind in the studio, hitting the streets with handbills, or at a "gig."

Juggling it all is possible. I have learned this fact through my own personal struggles, but there is a balance to be found for your finances and time that will aid you in finding success in your business/ministry as well as peace in your household. It will require some work on your part – which is usually the problem. When it comes to something we are passionate about or something "God told me to do," we tend to believe everything and everyone is supposed to fall into place and we won't have to work for it all. Get real. Your husband or wife is supposed to want your time and love and vice versa. He or she should be able to expect a certain amount of attention and compassion from you. Your spouse also should be able to depend on your contribution to the household, and should they express emotions about your lack in any of these areas, it does not mean they do not support you. Your belief in your ability to become a professional artist does not give you a license to belittle your spouse or guilt them into accepting whatever you are willing to give after you have given to your work.

I will never forget one artist I was associated with while in D.C. He was very talented and his production was on point. There are some artists you encounter very early in their ministry who sound the alarm in every one of your professional fibers as a future success. This was one such guy. He had what was needed to make it. He had the talent, the vision, the creativity, and the passion. He also had the willingness to invest in himself. The danger with a person so prepared and so ready is that they can tend to work ahead of divine timing, and also work in extremes. It is almost as if they have to prove they are ready so they push and push and grind and grind and keep moving and keep moving when truly, at this point, it is only God's timing that remains. He just had to be patient.

In a conversation with him one evening he decided he would pick my mind about his career and his position in the industry. He very much wanted to go into full-time ministry – right then. However, he had a wife and children to support and the music and ministering was not bringing in the money that would support them should he decide to go full-time. We discussed some of his finances and I fully believed there was a strategy he could implement that would allow him to go into ministry full time within a year.

You see, one thing I am when it comes to educating concerning this industry is consistent. I have for years counseled artists that if your desire is to work full-time then review your finances, find where you can cut unnecessary expenses or over spending, then pay your bills and mortgages or rent at least a year in advance. This way you can become a full time artist or minister and not be concerned about household finances for at least one year. You can solely focus on implementing your plan to become a financially and professionally successful artist, minister, or label.

I am not sure if he heard all I said or utilized selective listening, but this particular artist quickly saw where they could cut back expenses and became so motivated that he began the process at breakneck speed. Proclaiming God told him to go into ministry full-time he quit his job having little savings, moved his family from their house into an apartment, and began the struggle. The problem was God did not call for a struggle and I certainly did not tell him to quit his job.

Absolutely there are things that are revealed to us concerning the direction we should take during times of great struggle, but this was self-imposed rather than something orchestrated by God. His wife showed a very supportive exterior in public but anyone with minimal discernment could see she was going to break down emotionally any minute. If one of those church mothers with those "I know, baby" hugs came through, she would have sobbed in her arms uncontrollably. She was under much stress trying to hold it all together while her husband was off being an artist. Any word or appearance against his decision would have reflected negatively on her support as his wife. It should not be that way.

That entire situation never should have been that way. Had he been patient, continued to do what he knew to do and was doing as a rising artist, he would have continued to make the connections and gain the wisdom to be a successful name in this industry. Instead he, in my opinion, mistook his own desires for God's voice, missed the timing of God, put his family and marriage under needless strain, and to this day he has not become the national artist he had the potential to become. Fortunately after a couple years of struggling God opened the door to a full-time position in a church and, to my knowledge, the family is together and well today.

My point is that there is a high level of work, cooperation, and strategizing you will have to choose to participate in to find a successful balance between your ministry and your household. This is a challenge working moms have been facing for years. Success is possible. There is no blueprint to view and follow for success in this area. What works for one family and artist may not work for another. But consider making the family a part of your goals. Make them your team. Your music ministry/career is the family business.

So many artists spend time working on their "people" they miss the team that is in front of them. They need their producer and their DJ, and their armor bearer (security), and their personal assistant, their business manager, and their booking agent and on and on and on. Do you as an independent artist have so much business going on that you need a manger to give 20% of your earnings? Do you have so many performance requests coming through that you need a booking agent to give 15% of your money? Once your project is complete does your producer need to continually be by your side? And really how many frantic fans are bombarding you that you need security? Please understand I am not making light of any of these positions. I utilize all of them at the appropriate times myself.

What I am suggesting is that there is no one better equipped to understand your temperament and immediate needs than your spouse. He or she would serve as a better personal assistant. Perhaps your mom, retired and sitting at home, has a schedule that can accommodate checking Internet requests or returning phone calls. As technology-savvy as children are these days, consider using one to design your web site and consult you on the next big thing you should implement to help your ministry grow as a manager would.

When you and your team go out to do your thing, you separate yourself from your family. Take them with you. Give your children an understanding of ministry and of what mom or dad do. Even teach them your trade. When you go out to perform bring them along, instilling the value of family support, as well as teaching them the proper way to carry and present themselves. After all, as you progress and more demands are made on your time in larger public arenas you want your children to understand how to behave in certain situations.

By the time she was five I was able to take my daughter to interviews, concerts, even grand award shows, and though she had a tendency to sing continually, she also knew how to sit and have a conversation like a lady. She knew how to shake hands and introduce herself. She was not one of those children rolling around on the floor, playing with her dress over her head. Each age has its challenges but the children respond to your training. In exchange for her best effort at professionalism during the time mommy had to work, a special evening or the next day was set aside to do whatever she wanted and I would behave the way she needed from me – which often meant dirty at the playground or elbow deep in cheese pizza. "Train up a child" involves more than just making sure they are in church and know who Jesus is, but also education in finances, society, etiquette, and business.

Concerning your spouse, let me share my experience with you. When I was married my husband did not know or understand the industry. He never gained an understanding and came to resent having to hold the baby in the back of the church while I gave my attention to an audience full of strangers. By no means was that the downfall of my marriage but it certainly served as a point of contention and I have heard similar testimonies from far too many in this industry. Find a way to involve your spouse. Perhaps he or she is better with financial records than you and can serve as your accountant, or he or she is great with scheduling and can serve as your booking agent. Whatever the strength, infuse it in your process. When you make your passion their passion as well, they have as much of an emotional investment in it as you, and you will find working together is better for the ministry and your relationship than working apart.

STRATEGY

Though there are many aspects you cannot control – such as anointing and God's divine timing, there are many that you can. You can control your money, your production schedule, your marketing and promotion, but having control over all those aspects and more in your ministry is useless if you do not have a plan – one that details how and when you intend to implement phased actions. You must have a strategy to achieving your success; a plan and a timeline.

It takes a minimum of six weeks and up to six months or more to get a good song added on radio; an artist can be in the studio for three months to a year; there must be a sustained repetitive campaign to brand your name and image in the mind of consumers; and certain times of the year are better-suited for project releases than others. You need to take these points and more into consideration when designing your strategy. Even if you hire someone like myself to develop the best strategy for you to follow, he or she still will ask you many questions centered on these areas and more.

The goal is to organize the answers in such a way that will maximize your results. For example, you may plan to be in the studio from early October to Christmas. While in the studio you may find it advantageous to begin a pre-release promotional campaign to get the industry familiar with your name and image. Come December after a single has been picked, you may choose to release that single to radio for consideration while your project is being mastered and packaged. At this point you may decide to continue your pre-promotion stage of marketing and promotion, perhaps with EPKs (electronic press kits) and mailings announcing your first single and promoting your release date. According to your strategy you may estimate your single impacting radio around the Easter season to coincide with your release date, which gives you three months to stack your radio rotation adds. After kicking into your release stage of promotion you might begin scheduling a series of interviews and planning a promotional tour in the most receptive portions of the country and on and on and on. The point is to have a road map to your success.

There are a few industry keys to consider when developing your strategy. First, set stages. It is easier and more motivating to reach and complete smaller goals. If your sole goal is to be a superstar, well you may never reach that or it may take an unbearably discouraging long amount of time to reach it. However, if you have a pre-release plan, release plan, and post-release plan, for example, then successful completion of each stage will mean you have reached a goal and can continue to the next milestone in your career. Also, learn the calendar of the industry. If you are planning to impact radio in November with your hot single that everyone needs to hear, you are delusional. The radio industry, specifically, all but shuts down to new music in November (after Thanksgiving) unless it is of a holiday nature. Your song likely will not get in anyone's rotation, so that needs to be considered in your strategy. That is why I always suggest that artists put at least one Christmas song on their initial project. Programmers are always looking for new and original Christmas music, amid the multitude of "Silent Night" renditions. You will get the spin and everyone will need to revisit your CD at least once each year.

Likewise, artists that win awards get an extra boost of longevity on play lists. So if you release a single or project during the awards season, for example, it likely will go unrecognized. That is something that bears consideration but you cannot if you are not familiar with the industry calendar. One more thing, be flexible. Though you create this plan you must allow for adjustments in the industry, the consumer market, and your own personal life.

I have a real example of how good strategy combined with a good product can equal success. In January 2008 I attended the Stellar Awards in Nashville, Tennessee. I am not an industry events junkie so I kept my activities limited to the secondary awards ceremonies since my station was nominated for Station of the Year, and also to the artists/announcers networking luncheon. That is where I met up with many artists and aspiring artists as well as with my fellow colleagues who I only get to see at such industry events. The world has been made much smaller through telephone and e-mail which, though convenient and efficient, is still rather impersonal. During the networking luncheon I saw Regina Belle. I remember seeing her and thinking, 'I guess she's serious about being a gospel artist.'

Her single "God Is Good" was released to radio during the Christmas season some weeks prior to the Stellar Awards ceremony. I remember meeting her label owner, Ruben Rodriquez, in my office just before her single came in the mail. He told me that he had this song by Regina Belle that I absolutely needed to hear. By this time the music industry in general realized the gospel market was an additional consumer market open to secular artists who offered at least one inspirational single on their project. I immediately wrote our passing conversation and the single off as one such opportunity. Seeing her at the Stellars solidified her status as a full-fledged gospel artist, and her forthcoming project as more than just an inspirational CD.

As much of the nation did, I entered her song into light rotation, increasing spins as its popularity grew. By her CD release in May 2008 she was in heavy rotation across most of the U.S., crossing multiple formats, and climbing the charts.

On a promotional stop in New York she made her way to my radio station for the standard production work and interviews. At that time I had an opportunity to have a more in-depth conversation with her label owner, Ruben.

We talked about how pleased he was with her gospel industry acceptance and success, how everyone was embracing the single, and how he was finding it difficult to pick the next single. That was probably because there was absolutely no rush to. "God is Good" still had much shelf life in it. It was at this point that we began to discuss strategy. Of course Ruben is an experienced industry exec though this was his first run in gospel. I told him I thought his label's timing and execution of this project was perfect.

The single was released during the Christmas holiday season of 2007. Usually a no-no, this timing allowed the industry to become aware of Regina's re-entry to music and curious enough about the single to jump on it immediately after the last "Silent Night" was played. Slowly it emerged on playlists throughout the country. The night of the Stellars was the first large gospel music industry public event of the year and served as excellent pre-release promotion.

The push and promotion continued through the first quarter of the new year – which is traditionally commercially fruitless. During this time most of the consumer market is recovering from the over spending of the holidays, therefore pushing a project for purchase would be useless, but preparing its forthcoming retail success through increased airplay and continued promotion is beneficial. That is what the label did. By the time the CD was released in May 2008 it was in the top 20 on most charts and hit the top 10 on a few. Ruben fully expected the single to hit #1 in a couple of months and believed that the project would continue to fly off the shelves. Also figured into the timing was the single's continued exposure and popularity climb right into the soon-approaching voting period for the upcoming awards shows. There was no reason for Regina's label not to expect to grab multiple nominations and awards for this debut gospel project. It was in the plan for its success, and the strategy was executed effectively.

You or someone you have enlisted to represent you must have a plan for your success. There must be an estimated timeline and stated goals to meet during your process. You must have a strategy to execute effectively for your success.

HUMILITY

When you set out as an independent artist, behaving as your own label, you must utilize a certain quality, the lack of which can delay success and limit industry exposure. That quality is humility. The opposite of humility is pride. Pride will prevent you from asking questions. Pride will cause you to believe you know it all. Pride will make you believe you can make it by yourself. By humbling yourself and remembering Who you represent you open yourself to the knowledge and people who can assist you in achieving your goals. Most importantly you open yourself to being used by the Father.

He cannot get done through you what He wants done in the Earth with you in the way. You cannot get accomplished professionally what you want to accomplish either with you in the way. If you knew all the information you would already be the success you aspire to become. In fact, you would not have a need to read this book.

Lack of humility is the main barrier to success. A popular cliché in the gospel industry is "Sometimes artists block their own blessings." I have known independent and nationally-signed artists who got so high on themselves and the arrogance of who they viewed themselves to be that their labels have given up on them. Once the representative of the artist is no longer supporting them or once the artist's behavior make them difficult to support, we, in media, pull back. We begin to scale back airplay, personalities limit promoting them during their shows, promoters do not want the hassle so they book them less and less; all in all the positives that should follow become squelched by the attitude and mindset of the artist. That is a heart thing that no one can change but the artist. It is a small change that can yield great results on either end of the spectrum of success.

Also in the area of humility an artist must know not to compare themselves, their music ministry, or their professional success to any other artists. You are not Kirk. You are not Fred. Kirk and Fred could be the world renowned Franklin and Hammond or the independent Johnson and Wilkins from your city. They have their paths and you have yours. You can not determine your progress by their measure of success.

There was an artist I knew who wrote her own music, owned her own studio in her home, produced her own tracks and duplicated CD after CD for the public to love. Unfortunately, she did not have anything for radio to love or for the mainstream to love or even for the gospel consumer to love. Her sound did no match with the current music trends of the time, and her production quality just was not the best. The problem was this artist was completely sold on her brilliance and truly believed everyone else was wrong. Everyone in the industry was just hating on her and playing a big politics game that she was not going to play. None of that was true.

The music truly was not the best. It was not the worst but it would never meet its potential because of the artist's lack of humility. She wrote every song, produced it in house, recorded it in-house, duplicated it in-house, and gave it to the industry with a "now play it" arrogance. The door was never open for another more experienced producer to pull out untapped vocal potential, for a writer to bring a fresh sound, or even for an industry professional to bring their professional relationships toward any success for her projects. She refused to pay any money to an independent promoter and even started a tracking business herself. Of course that could not be successful because she never established the needed industry connections.

To her advantage she had quite the mind of an entrepreneur and I witnessed firsthand the effectiveness of some of her promotion and marketing creativity. Of course she had to be creative, by necessity. She shut out everyone who could have offered any traditional means of promoting her projects. She knew best and it was her way or no way. To date it has been no way. She has found very minimal commercial success locally and none nationally. The bulk of her financial success is tied to renting out her studio to other artists. It is a very unfortunate and unnecessary situation for an artist who still has the potential to be a great artist. But only if she learns to be humble.

You as a label and an independent artist cannot do it by yourself. Your success is connected to someone else's gift and professional abilities. You must be willing to seek and receive help. Furthermore, you do not know everything. Those who have been in this industry for 20 or 30 years will admit they do not know everything. Times change, trends change, and technology changes, all affecting the technique and strategy of operating in this industry. What those who have been around do know is how to navigate and continue in spite of, increasing their longevity. Your humility will help you access that wisdom – establishing and eventually leading to your continued success – or else your pride will precede your fall.

Chapter 6

EVERYTHING MARKETING

When you think of marketing remember that it is all about its root word: market. The market refers to the people your product services. Without them you are nothing, and I am not speaking in the awards show shout outs way. Literally, without a consumer base spending money there is no successful commercial recording career. When the market begins to suffer financially, or if consumers stop buying for any reason, the entire cycle of the industry is thrown out of whack. There is no money circulating between retail stores, radio and media, the record labels, or the artist. You must utilize effective marketing and meet the ever changing needs of your consumers in order to be successful commercially.

Within the field of marketing there are many elements. If you have taken a basic marketing course or read "Marketing for Dummies" you perhaps are familiar with the 4 P's. They are product, price, placement, and promotion. For the purpose of gospel artists I always add a fifth "P" of packaging. Though many view that as a sub-category of product, it is such an important area for recording artists, especially independents that it deserves its own place. A strategy on how you will manipulate these elements to yield the greatest must be determined prior to you jumping in the studio to record. Here are some specifics to help you understand the importance of each area.

PRODUCT

This is it. This is what you have to sell. This is what will bring you income. This is what will help you establish longevity: the product. The CD project is the product that is the end result of the recording process. It is not the end all to everything you will need to accomplish, but it is a vital part to activating many of the other areas discussed in the book as well as a tool in achieving your personal goals. The product, in every sense of the word, needs to be quality. We will discuss the external quality, or packaging, later. But the substance of the product has to be quality.

If you had your beat and recorded it in your Casio keyboard, then transferred it over to a basic audio program on your computer, the overwhelming majority of laypeople would agree that it is not the best quality. If those who are not industry-savvy would say that, how do you believe those who are in the industry would feel? You perhaps chuckled as you reminisce bopping to beat #3 programmed into your 80s keyboard, but this is what many of your colleagues submit daily for airplay consideration.

I often feel like Simon from "American Idol" as I wonder if a particular artist was serious when they mailed or gave me a CD. What in the world were they thinking? The static, or the hollow echo sound of the studio recorded on the track, or the classic microphone-in-the-bathtub quality are in no way equal to the quality of their favorite song on the radio. How could they believe they could achieve airplay with that product? And as for the actual content recorded on the product, what were they hearing? I also often feel like Simon when it comes to the quality of the performances as well. My goal is not to be rude or discouraging, but I have to be realistic when considering a commercial music endeavor.

There are some things I have learned to accept in music ministry. Many artists are satisfied entirely with only the support of their mom and church, and every song, no matter how commercially unappealing, is someone's favorite song. My very first Program Director, Winston Chaney, taught me that. Accepting these truths I again remind you that I am not speaking to those who just enjoy performing music as a hobby or for their local community or church, but rather to those who are seeking commercial and professional success.

If that is you but the studio you have chosen to record in is not quality or it literally produces a sound reflecting its location in the basement, the success of your product will suffer greatly. Choose a studio that has a history of quality recordings and a recording engineer that can present you with recent recordings as a representation of his/her talent for you to examine. The right engineer who understands the manipulation of sound into audio is so important. Cutting corners and going with promises rather than proven results can produce inferior results.

Likewise, if you have a desire to attain commercial success but your vocal skills are completely unappealing to the ear then the quality and value of your product will never achieve professional status. It seems harsh when put directly but let me tell you, there is a reason I do not have a CD out. Not because I do not know label owners that will sign me. Not because I cannot hold a note. It is solely because I understand the level of talent and skill needed to progress and survive as a professional artist. I have not been called to the ministry of music in that respect. Notice I did not say I was not gifted to sing. As I said I can hold a note like many of you. But beyond being gifted, in order to secure a successful product, you must be called. Had I been or if I am called to that in the future, I would implement exactly what I am advising you. Get a producer.

There are many independent artists who are musicians as well. For that reason they believe they are skilled enough to know and implement what is needed to produce a successful product. The most talented musician who has never been a successful professional recording artist likely has no idea what is needed or accepted by radio and the consumer market. If you have been solely focusing on mastering music that progresses a worship service, then you have not been mastering translating that experience into what will work for a recording project. You need a set of ears that has.

I will never forget when I found out one of the most successful projects by Hezekiah Walker, *20/85 The Experience*, was recorded in a studio. Had I read the liner notes thoroughly it would have been obvious. No where is there a church thank you note or a "recorded live at" mentioned within the liner. His hits "Grateful" and "Faithful is Our God" were both recorded in a studio with musicians and singers. No audience to feed from. No live applause. Pastor Hezekiah Walker had become a master at capturing and expressing the live church experience on a product for the consumer to enjoy. Interestingly enough, after 20 plus years of performance mastery he still worked with an additional set of ears and another perspective to ensure the best quality. He worked with a producer and it paid off big.

If you are just a vocalist, you need someone who can stop the tape and correct your enunciation, someone who can punch you in to strategically hit a high note and climax the song, or someone who can help the arrangement of your vocals and music flow to create the perfect atmosphere for your consumers. You need help. With time and experience you may get to the ranks of J. Moss and Fred Hammond. You will be able to go into a studio, do what you do, and submit it for release. But remember they have parent labels, so even when you get to that level of professionalism there is still someone at the label, on your promotions team, or with your distribution company with different ears that may ultimately turn the end result away as unacceptable.

In addition to seeking a producer, seek a vocal coach. In discussing instrumentalists with saxophonist Kirk Whalum, he expressed that one of his biggest peeves is when musicians do not study their craft. They never seek to better their skill. They stop lessons. They do not learn to read or write music. They are not well-rounded professionals who are masters of their craft. They simply know how to play. I have that same peeve with vocalists. Most lean too heavily on their talent or gift and they never develop their skill. How many gospel artists do you know with vocal coaches? There are not many professional or independent ones. When mucus begins to collect do you know how to clean your instrument (known as your vocal cords)? As an athlete takes care of his body by stretching before a workout, do you know how to warm up properly before singing an entire concert or service? Have you learned how to increase your range, or do you possess the same range and vocal quality you had your last decade of singing?

When you invest in yourself you are investing in your product. For a higher quality product you need higher-quality content. That starts with you. This brings me to another aspect of the product that commonly is lacking. Many independent gospel artists have tunnel vision. They view the product solely as the CD and what is on it. That limited vision will yield limited financial results. The truth is the product is you.

Your story, your life experiences, what brought you to Christ, and what influenced your music ministry are all fuel for the fire of your success. All that and more represent additional options for exposure, publicity, financial gain, and of greatest importance, ministry. At the beginning of this section I mentioned the CD project as the end result of the recording process. It is product in the sense that it is something to sell, true; however if that is all you have to sell then you will go through great periods lacking productivity and financial gain when you are between recordings projects. If you change your mindset to understand that YOU indeed are the product, then the list of things to sell are limited only by your creativity.

There was an artist I shared a manager with once. He could sing and his music was marketable. He worked very hard to position himself to sing in front of the top names and share the stage with notable artists and move CDs. He and his management were dedicated to achieving success with his project. What I attempted to convince them of was that his testimony was of greater value than the CD and the success of sharing the testimony would drive the success of the CD as well as open doors to spiritually and financially lucrative speaking and ministry opportunities. You see, while he was now a Christian singing gospel music, his experience was that he grew up Muslim singing R&B. Post 9/11, that testimony is the kingdom victory the American church loved to rally behind. As a former PR person I could easily envision the interview opportunities and massive exposure. The number of invites to conferences and conventions would be exorbitant. He could teach ministries methods of evangelizing other faiths. His name would ripple through the church community. But it did not. He and the manager chose to stay the course with the project which, unfortunately, never made an impact on the charts.

Take the blinders off and – without straying away from the ultimate purpose God has for your ministry – utilize other aspects of YOU to achieve your goals. This often is a difficult area for artists because artists of all kinds typically hide behind their art. That is the way they express themselves without explaining themselves. So a painter can hide his confusion in a mixture of reds and browns running together on a canvas. A designer can express their moods in her accessories and color combinations. And a gospel vocalist can mask his hurt over childhood abuse or divorce or their state of loneliness by pouring their emotion into the performance of a song. The difficulty is catching that same artist in an interview where they are transparent about the true influence of their lyrics. While it is good to be prepared and professional in interviews (to be discussed later in this chapter), there are parts of you that can connect with an audience that your music may not connect with.

Perhaps your connection is not through your life experiences or your testimony. Perhaps it is with the intimate apparel you designed to meet your personal needs, but other full figured saints can benefit from. Perhaps it is the how-to you have learned concerning conducting a worship service. Maybe it is what you learned about bringing down your blood pressure without medication. Whatever that additional part of you outside of music is that is relatable, consider it as another extension of your product, you, and once determined that this is something the Father would be pleased to use, implement it into your plan.

Whether that product is a CD or your testimony, never leave an audience without a piece of you. Have product everywhere you go. I managed a female rapper for a period of time and we had an opportunity to minister out of town. For outreaches and true ministry opportunities, you sometimes will find the ministry inviting you has no budget. While the opportunity itself will not yield financial gain through an honorarium, product sales have the potential of equaling the desired honorarium.

The problem was this particular artist's CD was not yet available. So to take advantage of this out-of-state opportunity and an audience we may never see again, we had to become creative. There we were, two creative (yet broke) sisters trying to generate gas and snack money for the road trip. We went to the local office supply store and purchased clear adhesive laminating sheets and from our own stash of office supplies we utilized heavy paper and hair ribbons. Out of these modest materials we created elegant and inspirational bookmarks. There were empowering phrases, lyrics, scriptures, and most importantly, e-mail and contact information on each bookmark. We sold them for $1 each and completely sold out.

Through developing a new product we were able to see financial gain were there was none, achieve a level of promotion, and build a tangible audience base to access for future product and performance efforts. Please strive to a greater quality product than our last minute bookmarks. Perhaps have your bookmarks professionally manufactured. Consider having the local Kinko's print a limited amount of tracks or pamphlets that offer your testimony and the wisdom you gleamed from it. Or work to have that all-important CD project at the ready. Stretch your creativity and utilize your resources to offer a commercially undeniable and kingdom-effective product.

PRICE

You, as an independent artist, are in the rare position to call the shots as it relates to you as the product and to your CD project. The signed artist you see on all the awards shows, at every event, and all throughout media is not given that opportunity. More times than not they are told by their label they need to be available for this promotional event or to perform at that show or travel on this tour – of course, all to the benefit of the label.

In addition, if you are popular in an economically depressed area where a $10 CD would move faster than one for $18.99, you have the ability to make that adjustment the signed artist does not. The retail price is the retail price. You as an independent artist also have the benefit of strategizing so that your profits exceed your initial investment. By spending less in the studio or streamlining your promotional plan to target regions rather than the entire nation you can utilize your finances more effectively. You have the benefit of knowing and the luxury of manipulating your expenses to deliver a $10 CD if you choose, moving units and maximize your profits. The average signed new artist does not have the choice of $50/hour mastering or $1,500/hour mastering (more in Chapter 9). You do. You should keep such things and more in mind when considering how much you will charge for you as the artist and for your CD project to recoup your financial investment.

Expenses & Distribution

Your list of expenses can range from three to five to an infinite number of costs to cover. That list is for you to make. Just keep in mind, anything, and I do mean anything you spend money on to benefit your business is an expense. "Anything, Denise?" YES! Anything from the paper clips you purchase to the duplication of your project. Purchase a new dress for a performance and that is an expense. Spend a tank of gas driving from store to store to stock your CD and that is an expense. You do not need to keep track of these expenses solely for tax purposes (keep all receipts), but you also need to plan expenditures and track them.

Whether you choose to purchase the $2.50 gel ink comfort grip pen over the $0.50 Bic is completely your choice. Just understand that you will need to find an additional $2.00 for the expense, as well as recoup the cost through your product and those things that make money for you. That may include your CD project, your performance fees, your endorsement monies, and any sponsorship dollars. Somewhere in there you will need to bring in the extra $2.00 that went out for that pen. Now apply the same concept to your actual expenses.

Preferably, apply the previous concept to your actual expenses prior to spending. I have witnessed many independent gospel artists, myself included, get caught up in the hustle. You rip and run to make that quick buck to keep the artist machine moving. The extent of the financial planning is to figure out how much one can afford to take out of the next paycheck to get in the studio or have CDs pressed or get handbills made. There is never truly an accounting to know all that has been spent or whether an equal or greater amount has been returned. I remember getting so proficient at the hustle that I could determine through pre-performance research (of the audience type and amount I expected and the event location) exactly how many DVDs I would need to sell after a performance of my one-woman play. If I needed an extra $300 for a bill or household need, I planned to move at least 15 DVDs at $20 each. If at the event it appeared to be a slow night then I would adjust the price to $15 or even $10 and work to sell the additional units needed to make up the difference. I could not leave without my goal plus the performance fee or I risked binding my personal finances. Poor business practices like that make an artist virtually no different from a drug dealer moving rocks for cash on the corner. It's a daily hustle of robbing Peter to pay Paul, and that is not the definition of success. God calls us to a place of excellence even in the business of ministry.

When considering what you will charge the consumer for your CD you must have an account of your expenses. If you, at a performance or online, are not the direct vehicle for a consumer to purchase your product you also need to consider two additional areas. They are your distributor and retail outlets.

The basic progression of music revenue is as such: the label sells a unit to a distributor for a price (assuming both are not owned by the same corporation). The distributor sells to retail for that price, plus their cut or percentage. The retailer then adds their cut atop that price and passes it to the consumer. What started out as a $3 CD will end up retailing in Wal-Mart for $18.99. What does this have to do with the price you set? Remember, we are talking a distributor now. You are not the direct source anymore. Now, the same disc you would have sold with no middleman for $20 may yield you $5. By the time the distributor sells it for $13 to the retailer and the retailer to the consumer for $18.99, your CD will once again be worth $20 but in this case you do not benefit. Paying for a $2.50 pen out of $20 seems a lot easier than out of $5 doesn't it? The logic is that with a distributor you ultimately will be able to reach more consumers and move more units causing your initial loss as an independent to eventually balance out. Unfortunately that is not always the case.

Aside from your personal expenses, when considering a distributor you must research where they distribute in the country as well as the chain outlets with whom they have agreements. If there is an agreement with Wal-Mart, for example, you need to know if they sell that distributor's catalogue as $10 value savers. That could work to your favor in one respect as consumers who are in tough economic times are quicker to grab a $10 CD than one for $18.99. As a commercial artist, moving many units at a value in a major retail outlet is not a bad look and can assist you in future business and industry endeavors.

Just a side note, many distributors and retailers have begun leaning to the "value saver" agreements that will help move product. Understanding the mind of consumers is a good skill to have. You see, though a consumer will hesitate to purchase an $18.99 CD, they will see extra value in purchasing two $10 CDs, which ultimately will cost them more money but will likewise help the distributor claim a greater number of units sold. It is value perception.

In the case of most independent artists much of this will not concern you. Distribution from a distributor that favors independents like Central South, for example, will yield minimal results without a promotion component. If retailers order your product it will sit without consumer awareness. Seek a P&D deal (promotion & distribution) that extends beyond just filling retail requests of basic distribution into promotion of the product as well. Unfamiliar projects and artists have a difficult time selling and a short shelf life. Distribution is a key to the commercial success of an independent gospel artist. You must have a vehicle for getting your product into the hands of consumers. Know the price both you and they will have to pay.

Retail

The independent artist's friend is local retail. You must have a relationship with that Christian book and music store in your area. Chances are, especially in urban areas, they are independent as well. Without a parent corporation to provide the necessary marketing, establishing a relationship with you is as important to them as it is to you. They need your following to visit their establishment and you need an outlet for your product to be available to the public. You will learn throughout this book as well as throughout your career the concept of "mutually beneficial." Radio airplay is based on whether your music will help a station, not on whether you have a great song (Chapter 7). Your calendar being booked depends on if you can pull a crowd, not on if you can stand and sing in a microphone. And your ability to gain and maintain shelf life may depend on the perception the retailer has of the potential economic success of your music.

Once you have established a relationship with a retailer they will likely offer you a consignment deal. Because you have not been proven they do not want to take the investment risk of spending their money to order and purchase your product from a distributor, yet they still want to benefit from any success it may have. With a consignment agreement you are allowed to set your product price. This is where you must again consider all we have discussed. No matter what price you set, the percentage you owe the retail establishment remains the same. For a 60/40 agreement on a $10 CD they will take $6, for example. From a $20 CD the retail cut is $12, and so on. Many retailers have their consignment terms set and are not open to negotiations. I have known some independent retailers to want as much as 70% and others as little as an even 50/50 split.

You must keep this information in mind along with your personal finances and your audience, when setting your product price. Remember, you have expenses to cover and (prayerfully) a profit to turn also. Moreover, consider any coupons or promotional campaigns you may run that will affect your product price. If you offer a $2-off coupon for a particular store where you have a consignment agreement, that $2 off comes out of your portion of the split unless otherwise negotiated. That is $2 less revenue to help counter your expenses. This is information you can know going in. You do not have to learn everything by doing. Use wisdom and prepare accordingly.

If the retailer you are considering is not independent but part of a chain, consignment may not be an option. However, if your product is quality enough to support the investment, it may be worth the effort to travel and meet with the regional buyer or president of merchandise about supplying your product. Similar to your actions with radio, you will find that leaving Detroit for a sit down with a company president in Kansas may yield greater results than an impersonal telephone call.

Performance

As you begin to regard yourself overall as a product with a determined value, you must consider other areas that may need price determination. "Other areas" can include a multitude of things such as consulting, back-up singing, preaching, teaching workshops, song-writing, etc. The main area that affects every artist no matter their additional aspirations, however, is performing. Your price will directly reflect your value. Your value is determined by your popularity or, better still, by your ability to draw an audience.

I make a distinction between the two because there are many artists who are well-known and popular, even legendary in the gospel music industry but who can not draw an audience of thousands on name alone as they were once able to. Therefore your ability to draw an audience above your personal popularity will determine your current monetary value, though popularity is an influence.

A flat rate is never suggested. The phrase "strike while the iron is hot" is very relevant to this subject. If you are fortunate to have radio support and media exposure in a particular market, you are of greater value there and can request more than perhaps in your home territory, where you are either saturated, do not receive as much support, or valued less as a performer. It is important to be flexible and adjust your rates to achieve the greatest financial outcome without missing or jeopardizing opportunities.

Likewise, there may be times when, because you are attempting to achieve support in a market or area, you may need to avail yourself at no cost to a church or promoter. In this case the opportunity itself is where the value lies.

I recall one day at a music workshop seeing an artist with a t-shirt that read "WILL SING FOR FOOD." That passion is needed in this industry. However, please know your time, energy, and skills have value, and though value perception may change, there is a monetary number that may, can, and should be attached whenever possible. Weigh carefully what you feel your worth is within the reality of your current industry standing, attractiveness to audiences, and quality of product to determine the price you will charge for your product: you.

At some point, while trying to maintain balance between your life and ministry, it may become a numbers game. I once had a friend who was a Christian DJ and one of the top to ever spin holy hip-hop. He knew he needed to make at least $2,000 a month to begin the move toward full-time ministry. He was on the grind to say the least, taking every gig he could come across. It was not uncommon to have a weekend completely booked. The problem was that folks were paying $300-$500 for his services. For a singer or rapper that perhaps would be a good start to things, particularly if the calendar stays booked. But for a top DJ it is different.

There is heavy equipment to transport and carry in and out of venues. While singers can arrive minutes before an event, DJs have the additional time of set-up and sound checks, not to mention packing up well after the congregation has left the building. That is a lot for a few hundred bucks. This particular DJ found himself frustrated with the reality of the amount of time and energy exerted and the minimal financial return, and the fact that the number of gigs he would have to work to meet his goal continually took him away from his wife and kids.

In advising him I tried to help him understand this numbers game I just mentioned to you. He was fortunate to have an established following and a regular flow of references and date requests. He had marketing and branding efforts underway, an Internet presence, and the quality of his services was worth more. If rather than accepting three $300 dates and two $500 dates in the month he accepted two $1,000 dates or three $800 dates he would cut down the time away from family and increase his value. Needless to say he was apprehensive. "What if they won't pay that and I lose the opportunity?"

Perhaps you have had this fear as well. With each level you ascend to in this industry and in ministry there has to be a greater boldness and a confidence. This is not to be mistaken for arrogance. That is a toxin which leads to destruction. But boldness and confidence are building blocks.

As his perception of himself and what he brought to the exchange increased, so did his fee, his quality of clientele, his exposure, and his ministry. God elevated him from doing church youth nights for love offerings to touring worldwide with a Grammy-nominated artist. He still often chose to do the local church youth nights but not for the money or the grind. Through discernment he knew God desired him to continue that service. As opposed to just using his gift he focused, managed, and organized it into stewardship. Consider all things in considering your price.

PLACEMENT

Your placement is crucial to public perception of your importance as an artist. Admit it, if a local promoter asked you to open for his Donnie McClurkin concert your stock would increase in your own eyes, not to mention to the industry and your local audience. Your name on a flyer next to Donnie McClurkin's name is far better than your name on a flyer singing for Women's Day at your church. Of course you are grateful for both opportunities. What is greater in the McClurkin example is the placement. You are placed next to someone that has great respect and appeal, thus non-explicitly telling the consumer, 'I am worth it."

Professionally your goal is to get to that realm of respect and branding where others are made greater by being in the presence of your greatness through Christ. On the way to that place, it is important to place yourself as close to that perception as possible. As a performer your name next to others of greater value does help your value which will help your overall marketing goals. Likewise, your image next to others helps your promotional goals.

I remember when I got to a point in my radio career where all the hard work and effort manifested itself in actual value. I was a national personality and a known name. Suddenly taking pictures with everyone did not matter. When I first started I needed to have a picture with everyone I interviewed or bumped into for trade magazines, my web site, and personal promotion. With success I got to a point where I didn't have to work so hard and photos were not as important. I could enjoy the experience and if photos were taken it was mostly for the promotion of the artist or the radio station.

Before I got to that level, every minute was an opportunity and opportunity was taken. You should do the same. Do not forget all you learn in this book concerning building relationships. Every effort should be made to extend beyond the photograph and beyond the opening act opportunity.

Speaking of placement, though everyone has a role, the truly influential industry people are with the artist you are next to in the photo. Do not just get Donnie's number because you opened for him. His manager takes the calls for his performance dates and will be the one to suggest other acts that the promoter should pursue if asked. Not Donnie. The label rep next to him is the one that could get you a deal if you are seeking that route. Donnie will help elevate artists from within his camp.

I remember one artist told me how she pressed her way through the crowd like the woman with an issue of blood to get close to Kirk Franklin for a 20-second encounter where she gave him her CD and begged him to listen to it. How productive does that sound to you? I can tell you it was not very productive and, in fact, was an opportunity for the enemy to discourage her as she waited and waited for Kirk to call. Had she stepped to the side and talked with the unassuming gentleman walking quietly behind, she may have gotten further and had the mind to get a business card with a number and e-mail address for a follow-up opportunity. Understanding placement of everything and everyone in this industry is important.

Lastly we must discuss the placement of your project. Most record stores organize their inventory in alphabetical order and by genre. However, there are subtle marketing gimmicks that emphasize some artists over another and can influence the perception and purchasing choices of the consumer.

When you walk into a store your focus is drawn immediately to what is in the middle of the room as opposed to what is along the walls. Consumers are pulled to displays that demand their attention. I doubt if as an independent artist a retailer will allow you to place a display in the middle of their store. However, you may be able to offer a variation and take advantage of a consumer's line of sight. Rather than a large, middle-of-the-floor display, offer a small display for their countertop, particularly for your local Christian retail store. Just as you are prone to purchase that gum or hand sanitizer you don't need just because it is in your line of sight right next to the register, you may be able to increase your sales with a countertop display.

Please understand that if there is no radio support or consumer demand for your project this will not be effective and may hurt any such future proposals with retailers. Furthermore, it will shorten your project's shelf life. Do not attempt independently. This should be considered as a part of your overall marketing strategy. As your strategy begins to yield results please know those results will vary. You may be received in Indiana sooner than New York. Once again, be flexible. If Indiana is where you see results put your resources there and offer a display while continuing your efforts in New York, for example.

If you are fortunate to gain the popularity and demand all artists strive for you can seek to devise better placement agreements with retailers. Currently listening stations are the premium marketing tool of choice with retailers. They are positioned at the line of sight of consumers and demand attention. The quality of your project must be able to increase sales from a listening station where the consumer is able to preview it and make a purchasing decision on the spot. You want that decision to be in your favor. If your project lacks in quality at all I do not suggest a listening station. You may turn off consumers and lose sales. Let the packaging and local media encourage them to take a chance and purchase it.

You must have a strategy for your commercial success. The lack of one will place you in the least desirable place in retail, the value bin. I mentioned shelf life earlier. Much like there is an expiration date on bread and milk, there is an unspoken expiration date on your project. With new music being released every week of the year, no retailer has space on their shelves to keep music that is not selling. As an independent artist, particularly one with consignment agreements, if your product is not selling there is no need for a retailer to continue to dedicate shelf space to it. It will expire. Those with consignment deals will be asked to come in and pick up their unsold product and product ordered through a distributor will find its way to the value bin where it will be sold for a fraction of the cost in an effort for the retailer to recoup some of their investment.

This is one reason I suggest to many independent artists, do not put a copyright date on the back of your CD. This is particularly applicable to your first one. The reality is you may be working that CD across the nation for years. You do not want to give someone the perception that your work is dated or have them question its value before they listen because "1999" is displayed on the back cover. Yes, something as simple as the copyright date can affect your efforts. Everything must be considered when attempting to achieve the best placement possible for your product.

PROMOTION

A product is nothing without promotion. There must be a promotional strategy or plan developed within your larger marketing strategy. This is a concept many in the gospel music industry, particularly independent artists, fail to address prior to spending their entire budget in the recording studio – then their faith becomes challenged when what has been done for God does not prosper. You must have resources and a vision for your promotion.

A vocalist may have the most anointed voice and, having worked with the world's greatest producer, now has the "must-have" CD of the year. Without promotion no one, not consumers or media, will be aware of the project's existence and it will become commercially unsuccessful. The primary method of making consumers aware is through media exposure, specifically radio. The primary method of making media aware is through Industry Relations (IR).

Though IR is not officially recognized within the P's of Marketing it is certainly an aspect those most successful in the business of their industry quickly learn – in this case Christian entertainment. Much like PR, Industry Relations is a deliberate, planned, and sustained effort to gain a positive product perception – only in this case it is to key factions within that industry rather than the public – and works to establish an understanding of the product's contribution. The primary methods of making your industry aware are promotion and networking (or building relationships).

Exactly how you will promote yourself and/or your project is a significant part of your overall marketing strategy. The following chapter gives you most of the current information you need to know concerning radio. That particular medium is ever changing as the audience, systems of rating, and revenue streams change, therefore the way you promote to radio today may differ 10, 15, 20 years from now. However, much of what you need to understand concerning how best to strategize for maximum results for radio is available to you. The vast majority of independent gospel artists will not receive national radio play. A main reason is lack in the IR department.

The new indie who attends every conference, meeting people, conversing and establishing relationships with industry decision makers while also continuing to beat the streets for public awareness, selling CDs out of their trunk, and hitting every concert and promoter, etc., will likely have a more successful sophomore or follow-up project. I say follow-up and not first project for a couple of reasons. First, the true artist usually finds it difficult to not continue the creative process. While this relationship building and "paying your dues" process is under way, music trends change and artists mature and become eager to get back to creating. The sophomore project is usually more focused and contains fewer of the not-so-stellar elements that came through lack of knowledge and lack of guidance on the initial project.

Secondly, the "paying your dues" and relationship-building processes take time. If you are not engaging someone with immediate access to the industry decision makers and are solely working to promote yourself, it may be a few years before you are known, trusted, and see results. Within years you will likely have another release. Many of you reading this book already may have your first CD out and want that commercial success and industry acceptance that has eluded you outside of your local market. Let's discuss this issue of promotion further.

Success in promotion, like much in this industry, is limited only by your creativity and your product's relationship to its audience. If you understand how your product most relates to or connects with your audience you will discover the best ways to reach them through creative and effective promotional activity.

Axe is a brand name body spray for men. There was a time when body sprays were embraced solely by the female consumer. Most men did not have body fragrance as a priority and those who considered it achieved it primarily through cologne. That product of body spray had no connection to a male consumer base. So what changed? Those responsible for marketing this particular product changed the connection to the consumer from a smell-good, refreshing, beauty-enhancer for women to a chic-magnet, cool-tool, mist for men. The exact same body spray product, packaged differently and with a clear perspective for the audience to target opened a completely new consumer market and created a successful brand to build on.

It would benefit anyone attempting to market a product to research Maslow's Hierarchy of Needs. It essentially details the basic needs of man, building from the base of the greater needs like survival, food, shelter to the lesser needs of man like the need to feel desired. Whether the least or the greatest, a product's ability to connect with any need of the consumer will determine its ability to succeed commercially. Axe connected with a man's need to feel desired and a need for physical intimacy. What need does your product fill? I submit to you that if your only response to the question of what need your project fills is "It will bless you," then you are setting yourself up for disappointment.

First, from a spiritual perspective God has designed you and your ministry to reach a particular group of people. You have souls assigned to you and they are not just anyone who does not know Jesus or anyone with ears to hear your CD. We, as the body of Christ, have got to start taking our individual assignments more seriously and stop trying to be the one for the masses.

Do not misunderstand, there are those set aside to speak to the nations but they are a select few, and while those who are not called to that are continuing to aspire to reach those souls, pockets of souls here, there, and everywhere go unreached. Those souls are just as important to the Father and if you make it to TBN or BET while the souls in Sacramento who were assigned to your account are never reached, I cannot image the Father saying, "Well done, thy good and faithful servant." A servant fulfills the requests of the master. Consult Him to determine what need you and your project are to meet. Meeting a need is the true definition of ministry.

A second reason for this focus is based in the reality of business. There are hundreds of thousands of gospel CDs available that will bless someone. We learned from "American Idol" there are hundreds of thousands of individuals that can sing, rap, or play an instrument. If you are just singing to bless someone, commercially you will suffer. You have heard and will continue to hear me question, who is your music for? This is a continuation of that discovery. What needs are you attempting to meet?

Though Shirley Murdoch's gospel music is enjoyed by all, her song "I Love Me Better Than That" revealed clearly the connection her product was making, and with which consumer. Hurt women seeking empowerment embraced it. Not only was the CD recording promoted in that direction, but Shirley Murdoch as a product directs the majority of her ministry towards addressing that need. From preaching, to teaching women's conferences, to stage plays, the connection to the audience is clear and consistent. She has branded herself effective in women's ministry.

In business a brand is a recognizable name or image that has established consumer loyalty and commercial success. When one speaks of commercial success most who do not understand business go no further than thoughts of money. Financial gain is but a part of commercial success. In branding you are building a name, reputation, and image, among other things. Repetition helps to burn such things in the mind of the consumer much like a physical brand burns an image into skin to identify livestock. This repetition is achieved through consistent and prolonged media exposure via press releases, radio, television, the Internet, print, and more.

Both positive and negative media exposure can help in branding. The person who would know the boundaries of both is your publicist. They have the understanding and industry relations to gain the proper exposure for your product. With most independent gospel artists publicity is at a bare minimum. The person responsible for promoting your music to radio for airplay likely will set up interviews and inquire about promotional appearances while they work your single, and only while your music is hot. The problems are that first your music will not always be hot, and secondly, you will miss critical exposure by looking solely to radio during this limited window of time.

I can feel someone reading that feels I am not talking about them. After all, you do not just focus on exposure from and through radio but you spent several hundred dollars on e-blasts and ads in the *Gospel Times* magazine, for example. Open your mind. There is a greater level and remember the way to be most effective is by practicing consistency and repetition. Trust me, whether or not you are receiving airplay there is a constant flow of new music for program directors to consider that will soon take attention away from your music. After attention shifts, you are an afterthought until you prayerfully have another single when much of your promotional efforts are again directed toward media professionals in hopes they will make the public aware. The repetition should include a sustained consumer-targeted effort as well. The public, like the industry, needs to get to know you and your music.

Music videos do help, but do you have the relationships to get your video played? Multiple televised interviews assist the effort but, do you have the connections to get booked? Radio, print, downloads, e-blasts, radio drops – anyway to get your name, image, ministry, and music into the mind of the consumer and the industry will work to achieve your overall goal of branding and ultimately professional longevity. But do you have the time and relationships to make it happen? A publicist who has mastered the art of exposure does. Consider adding a professional publicist to your team in addition to your independent promoter. If it is not completely within your budget to hire someone who has worked in the industry for 25 years, start off with a novice trying to build a PR business, a college marketing student, or your spouse. The initial goal is to gain exposure and that is a time-consuming process. If you have a clear vision and clear instruction you can utilize someone as your legs until you are in a position to work with the PR cream of the crop.

Your publicist, while focusing on media exposure, is looking to expose YOU as the product, making your music a part of you and not just looking to promote your CD. However, you do not want the music to suffer while your name and ministry become household. To ensure that the foundation of your music is solid and any current singles are exposed properly you will need, as mentioned earlier, an independent music promoter. They are independent because they are not employed to work exclusively with one label. They are independently available to work with any artist and they focus all their efforts and relationships on getting that artist's music played by radio. Some of their duties include suggesting the best single to push; they will track your music's progress; they work for you in securing radio station related appearances, and with scheduling on air interviews.

There are two main reasons to hire an independent promoter. First, to free up your time. It takes many hours to contact more than a thousand gospel radio stations nationwide just to ask about a CD or song. Please trust me when I tell you, they rarely get contact with a program or music director on the first call. It takes calls, call backs, messages, e-mails, and on and on. Even if a program or music director has scheduled tracking time, it is a brief window at a specific time of the week, and every promoter in the nation is attempting to contact a station during that same window. Promoting is a time-consuming necessity. In the following chapter I address your need to make time to contact stations yourself at some point, to help build relationships. But if overall, you do not have the time, hire a promoter.

The second reason to hire a music promoter is for access to their relationships. There are some promoters that I, both as a personality and a program director, have worked with my entire career. We have established a relationship that will in many cases yield immediate results. Because of our relationship, their reputation for working with hit-makers, and their access to resources when the station requests something, the music of an independent artist they promote will easily be considered before another artist who is unknown (and is being promoted by an unknown). In considering music from an artist of a familiar promoter, you can count on having justification should a PD choose to add their single into rotation. A promoter's professional relationships and effectiveness in achieving your goal of airplay become yours when you become their client.

Be advised, some independent promoters, publicists, and consultants are snakes who will continue to take on as many artists as they can, so they can get as many checks as they can simply because they can. They are running a business just like you. They will promise the world but fail to tell you that 1) your music is on a list with 10-15 other artists, and 2) they may only get a opportunity to discuss three or four artists with a busy PD. If you are not their priority you do not reap the benefits of those promises.

Too many times, promoters have reached me for tracking and inquired about the music rotation of three to five artists. The problem was they were taking checks from up to 15 artists, at least 10 of which I was never asked about. When one of those 10 call, thanking me for playing their music, I have the unfortunate task of revealing I was never asked about them and am not playing their music. Do not just trust the weekly report your promoter gives you concerning your music. Follow up with the station yourself. Though expensive, invest in monitoring software that allows you to see what each station in the nation is actually playing. Lastly, whenever possible hire a promoter, publicist, or consultant based on a referral from an artist who not only used them but also found a measure of success with them. Anyone can say, "I've worked with …," and offer a list of artists and years of exchanges. Check their integrity and go with the proven best.

During your promotional efforts you may have an opportunity to discuss your project, your ministry, and your music for the public. This will likely take place through an interview. In your professional grooming, take the time to study and train yourself in the art of interviewing. Ultimately time and experience will be your greatest teachers, but you can advance the process with personal knowledge. Here are some tips:

1. **Watch and listen to professional interviews as much as possible.** Celebrities have coaches who take the time to prep them and train them in how to be most effective during an interview. As an independent artist you may not have that resource. Take advantage of their training. Journalistic shows like "20/20" or "Primetime" are great for understanding how to listen and answer in-depth questions. Entertainment shows like "Access Hollywood" and "E! News" are good for learning how to interact in an active, time sensitive, yet casual environment. Listening to a variety of radio, not for entertainment but critically for understanding, is a good tool as well.

2. **Know and remember your purpose.** There is a time limit on the duration of an interview. Some interviewers can easily stray into entertaining conversation for several minutes, and before you know it your time has passed and your product promotion is minimized in a 10-second "Pick up the CD today," or "Log on to my web site." If your purpose is to promote your CD then make every bit of idle chatter lead back to that purpose. If a promoter of a concert has you interviewing to promote an event it is the same thing. I am not implying that you should monopolize or try to run the interview. That is a sure way not to be asked back. Just remember you are not there to hang out, but you actually have a purpose. Make sure it is accomplished.

3. **Know your facts.** In preparation for an

interview record labels and publicists swamp the interviewer with bios and press releases and music and more, so that he or she knows as much as possible about the artist prior to the interview. The behind-the-scenes truth is most of that material will never be reviewed. It might be glanced at for any compelling points but never truly reviewed. Particularly in radio, an interviewer knows the questions they want to ask. So while they should – and probably do – know you sang with such-and-such, or you received this award and worked with that producer, the questions will still be asked. You must know the facts of your experience, your ministry, and your music so you can properly and easily speak on it. Know what your music is about, who it is for, your inspiration behind key songs, your current single and your next single, and please know your event information and contact information. There is no excuse for an artist not to know his or her own web site address – and "um" is not a word.

4. **Be conversational.** Nervous or unsure artists make for a difficult and unproductive interview. Relax and have a conversation. That may prove difficult if you are not a "people person" by nature. If that is you, you will likely come off to the interviewer as boring and too much work to interview, having to pull answers and banter out of you. In that case, the interviewer will quickly get to the facts, promote your CD, and cut the interview short. In contrast, the conversational and pleasant artist is likely to be asked, "Can you stay around awhile?" and be kept through the next break and even asked back. Every personality has a list of artists they will be okay

with never having to interview again. Do not let that be you.

5. **Do not oversell yourself.** Whether you are promoting your CD on radio through an interview or at a vendor table in personal conversation with a consumer, watch the oversell. Make sure the information you give passes the "Who cares?" test. When an artist gets into the industry awards no one has heard of, and the number of spins in radio, and the video on the cable network the audience cannot access, and the concert that is sold out, and all the information that is unimportant in an effort to make the artist sound important, the promotion becomes hype. As one legendary rap group once said, "Don't believe the hype." Too much "you" is counterproductive and ineffective. It is perceived as borderline arrogant and it is a turnoff. If you and the CD are quality, others will clearly see the value even through your word economy, and your promotion will effectively meet its goal.

PACKAGING

How a product is visually put together for presentation to the consumer and industry has become an increasingly esteemed part of the process. Grammys, Stellars – many awards are dedicated to honoring those who have mastered the art. Most importantly, however, is how extremely influential a product's visual presentation is to its success. You will hear me, even in this book, repeat a popular and simple sentiment of the industry. "If it looks like crap it probably is crap." Feel free to substitute "crap" with whatever word makes you feel comfortable. Unprofessional…amateur…a hot mess – the sentiment remains.

Unfortunately in our American culture we have been trained to make snap decisions based on the exterior of a thing. It may be a restaurant with an elaborate exterior giving the expectation of a 5-star meal; a man with a black hoodie and dark clothing looking suspicious in the distance causing concern; or a CD project submitted for airplay with a faded picture printed on a home computer as the cover and a handwritten CD-R inside. In everything, the exterior communicates immediately something about how that object or entity should be valued. That exterior provides the first understanding of what something is worth and how it should be addressed.

Most respond to the first impression so it must be as captivating and intriguing as possible. As the saying goes, "You never get a second change to make a first impression." The very first thing they see that represents you must be golden. Since throughout this book we have dealt with you as the product, as well as with your CD project, for consistency we must briefly address your packaging as an artist.

I readily admit I am not the poster child for entertainment presentation. I did not have personal lessons in female grooming from any significant woman in my life. They pretty much left me to play sports and discover my own style. Through the years it has been just that for me, a discovery. Some days the treasure I find shines more brightly than on other days. But I did learn from a few people I consider friends in this industry that there is more in me than I display.

I can solidly say it was not the way I dressed, the make-up I wore, my hairstyle, trends I followed, or the way I flaunted my exterior that got me to the number one market, but truly the hand of God moving through my experience, education, and expertise. I worked very hard, and often used that as a cop-out for not taking the extra time to learn how to present myself and execute an image successfully. The interesting thing is that as God elevates you, there is no comfort in the things of the level you were elevated from. I can clearly remember moving from

85

sweats to jeans, and from jeans, to my first fly black pinstriped suit with the shadow gray stripes. I even remember moving from everyday sneakers to my crisp clean events sneakers to wedges, and finally to open toe heels (still not my favorite).

Clothing is not the end-all. A presentation must be complete from head to toe. This area still presents challenges for me, as any woman trying to find the right hassle-free hair for a busy schedule or time to squeeze in a mani-pedi can relate. Yet I still press and you should too. Help is needed in areas of ignorance. In other words, if you do not know, ask another who is a proven expert. Image consultants will help you discover and enhance your personal style; make-up consultants are available to teach you the proper way to utilize make-up and implement skin care (guys too). If your budget allows you to go to a professional just one time, use that as a learning opportunity, asking questions on how you can maintain this look on your own. That is how I became a master at eyebrows. Wax sessions at $15-25 a pop can add up. Where professionals are not readily available there are a slew of manuals and how-to books lining the shelves of every major bookstore chain. Ignorance is not longer a reason but an excuse.

There is not one audience within the gospel or Christian community that wants to see someone who looks like they rolled out of bed – or worse, slept on the street – take the stage to entertain or minister to them. The vast majority of audiences want to see, receive, and respond to a professional well put-together artist. Much like an audience is influenced by your first impression, a consumer is influenced by the initial appearance of your CD project.

Again, an audience can assume by an individual's appearance and personal presentation the extent of their professionalism and experience as an artist. A consumer strolling the isles of a retail store, or a program director sifting through mounds of mailings and CD submissions, will assume your project is or is not worth the time to purchase or review based on its appearance.

There is an art and a science to packaging a project. The art is in the design. The science is in the strategic placement of the design elements. Both must work together and do so according to the imaging goal set forth by you or your label. If you do not have access to an artistic director experienced in making critical packaging decisions, research what others have done before you. Find those projects that have received Grammys and Stellars for packaging and see how they position elements in relation to the artist or how they used angles or color. Work with what you have learned and design your project cover, liner, and back. But do not stop there.

Once you have completed the task to your satisfaction, find 10 people to serve as your unofficial focus group. Ask five people (non family members) and five industry professionals a series of questions. They can include: Is this attractive? If you saw this in a store would you buy it? What type of music do you think is on a CD with this cover? Ask as many questions as you need to get the feedback you desire in order to make the decision to make revisions or to go to press. If you try to get constructive comments from 10 people who know you and are unconditionally supportive of your ministry, you run the risk of being misled into packaging that missed its potential.

Creativity and a critical eye are key. If you want to yield results your visual representation must transcend beyond the five people in a group standing in a semi-circle in matching outfits with a pastel background or the choir on the steps of the church photo. Accentuate the positives and work to cover any negatives. For years Kelly Price and Kierra "Kiki" Sheard were just heads on their CD covers. Unfortunately, the entertainment industry continues to help perpetuate the culture's belief that full-figured is a commercial liability.

The overweight part of an artist often is off set by the warm playful smile and head tilt or the chin to eye shot. How about Musiq or the sister from Rizen? A strategic effort is made to rarely present them without shades or tinted glasses to cover their less- than-perfect eyes. The crazy thing is that these are solely stage and public presentation tactics. In personal settings it is just them.

Such manipulation of individual traits, fashion, and photo software work to create the perfect package, which reinforce the artist's image and further the marketing process. Moreover, the risk of the average consumer cruising the aisle of a record store being turned off by something contrary to our standard of beauty is eliminated.

The actual number of units sold or passed over merely because of packaging has never been researched. However, I am sure that like myself, you too have been caught in a complete waste of money. Perhaps you had some extra money to spend at the mall and stopped by the gospel section of the record store. You pick up a CD you have not seen before but you think you have heard or seen the artist's name once or twice. It's only 15 bucks and it looks like something you can get your praise on to. You purchase the CD and on the way home pop it into your car's player. It is pure disappointment, to say the least. From the energy the jeans-rocking artist exuded on the cover you thought this would have an urban flavor with some skate tracks on it only to find the title track "We're Having a Praise Party" is a slow quartet song.

That may be a bit of an extreme example, and nothing against quartet music, but this is real. At the end of the experience they have another unit sold, your money is gone, and you are stuck with a CD to sell on eBay. The look of a product, whether the product is you the artist or your CD, directly affects its commercial success.

If perhaps this portion on personal and product packaging seems a bit vain to you, I agree. It is on one hand. It is also considered "doing all things in excellence" to the spiritual one. Whichever stance you take you must remember you chose to be a commercial artist. You can go, as the Father leads you, and give away your music free of charge to whomever it will bless and very few of these rules will apply. But as long as you call yourself a professional artist and desire the respect and recognition that accompanies that position, you and all that is connected to you (CDs, e-blasts, personal assistants, etc.) must look the part. And as long as you count yourself singing, rapping, or playing for the King, you must appear worthy to be His representative.

Packaging is important. It is also important that you do not manufacture something artificial.

Remain true to the you you discovered in Part I of this book and the tool God created for His purpose, and present them in the best possible light to achieve success.

Chapter 7

<u>THE TRUTH ABOUT RADIO</u>

The days of breaking a song are over. The days of an artist connecting with a jock, slipping them their CD and that jock spinning it for the love of it are gone. The time when good music and even the expressed desire of the listeners dictating the local radio station's playlist has virtually disappeared. Those times have been replaced with quantitative music testing, national tracking of singles, and good old-fashioned industry networking. As the radio industry changes its ability to generate money, and its form of audience measurement are altered, so changes radio's programming and more specifically how radio companies decide to use music to achieve their financial goals.

You see, radio is like a big Monopoly game. Have you ever played with that person who purchases one of each group of property rather than the entire group? Their actions affect how you continue to play the game. You now have to change your strategy in light of the parameters set for you in order to be the most effective. There are elements of this entertainment industry where others' strategies have changed how radio deals with artists and how radio chooses which song will get airplay. The ones in radio who can learn, re-learn, strategize, adjust, and execute effectively will be the most successful with the greatest listenership and most profitable bottom line. This focus on the process and the strategic manipulation within radio often forces programmers to have tunnel vision viewing artists as pieces in the game.

The intimate relationships with a program director, music director, or personality are relationships that have been nurtured and developed over 10-20 years in this industry and they are few and far between. In fact, several such relationships have proven to be a liability with accusations of payola and favoritism, which further supports the current distance between radio and the artist. So what does this mean for you, the independent artist?

Consider this, what would you do if I told you before we started the Monopoly game that I was going to purchase one of every group of properties making monopoly success for you either costly or impossible? Would you have decided that you did not want to play with me before we began? Or would you have learned more about the game, maybe even developing another strategy that would be more successful?

I can tell you that major labels with major money have purchased a piece of each group of properties before you stepped foot in a studio. This was done to benefit their investments – their artists. Arbitron has taken a piece here and there through PPM by creating an atmosphere unfavorable to artists unrecognizable to the measured audience. Finally, that local personality you met at your church anniversary service that you gave your CD to has little to no power to select their own music for airplay, and you have no clue how to get to the person who does. Now all these challenges exist before you, and we haven't started playing yet. We are still deciding who will be the shoe and who will be the race car. So what are you going to do?

Please know, there is no space for arrogant, self-righteous egotism if you want to be commercially successful as a major artist. So "I don't need radio. I'll just do it out of my trunk or on the Internet" is not an option. Radio still moves units and exposes artist. However, if you have decided this is not for you and you do not have the time, energy, or calling to play this game I understand. Many try to till a bigger plot of land because of personal desires rather than what God has assigned them to or graced them for. There is a place for the local artist who has been called to bless their Jerusalem with their music ministry and no further. However, if you have been called to the uttermost and want to continue, I have information that will help.

There was a time in radio history when the jock controlled his show. He was hired because he was the voice that could connect with the audience, create the desired atmosphere on the air, and be a credible source to teach the community the hits among other cultural, community, and political information. Everything and everyone was touchable and approachable. Disc jockeys were so approachable that a label or artist with a song could approach a DJ and pay him to spin their record as many times as the money would stretch.

Needless to say this practice known as pay-for-play or payola, was abused. The same artists and labels began to buy all the programming time, squeezing out the little guy and producing an artistic uneven playing field. The practice was outlawed and more strategic and organized programming practices came into play. The science of it began to catch up with the art. This is when I entered the industry, back when you needed a license from the FCC to operate radio equipment. Strategies and practices have been altered or completely changed several times since then. Undoubtedly, the information given in the initial printing of this book will change as the industry continues to. That is why an ongoing digestion of the things of your trade is vital to your continued success. You must eat, breath, and sleep it.

This is true of any profession in life. The one who best knows and understands the rules and dynamics of the industry will find the most success. A runner who understands terrain, weather influences, footwear, and breathing will be more effective than the runner who only understands putting one foot in front of the other and running. The artist who understands radio, marketing, music and cultural trends, etc. will always have greater long-term success than the artist who can just sing. Please remember in this chapter we are talking about the industry (specifically radio), not your ministry. No matter how anointed you are, for commercial success you will need to understand and work within the practical rules of the industry.

THE PROCESS

Most independent gospel artists believe the way to gain radio play is to pull a list of radio stations, most likely from the latest issue of *Gospel Round-Up*, and begin mailings to stations throughout the nation. When these "packages" arrive on programmers' desks they are usually large envelopes full of material that is completely unnecessary and uninspiring.

The typical indie artist package is a folder, usually high-quality vinyl or plastic ones, commonly brightly colored and filled with anything relating to the artist. Within it is a bio, newspaper spotlight clippings, any chart positions photocopied and highlighted, reviews, playlists reflecting radio play at any and all radio stations, a DVD performance or concept video, a full CD project, and a radio sampler or single. More elaborate packages also may include some premium item like a t-shirt, poster, mouse pad, etc. When you add the value of the package contents with the adequate postage, each package is probably worth $25-$40 apiece. The average independent artists mail out 20-50 packages to the stations on their initial list, to say nothing of additional packages as they continue to meet industry professionals throughout the year. That is a pretty nice chunk of money out of your pocket. Even if you took paper and folders from your job or used their mailroom, you as the artist are still investing quite a bit of your finances.

Of the entire contents of the average independent artist's package – the bio, clippings, playlists, charts and any other papers – are all tossed. In most cases, the high-quality folders are kept for personal use (they are expensive) though there are several program directors who toss those as well. This is radio so the need for a DVD is close to non-existent. They, along with any singles or CDs we decide we do not need and will likely not add, are also either tossed or sent out with the street team as giveaways. Most program directors keep a full project and on the rare chance a single is chosen to be added, the single is sent to the production department and left to reside in the music library. Of the entire $25-$40 package most of it ends up in the circular file – also known as the trash.

I know many of you invest a great deal of time, effort, and money in the presentation of your music ministry. To hear that some program or music director most likely will just throw the bulk of it into the trash and toss the CD in a pile somewhere near their desk can be a bit disheartening. Take courage. There is a place for that elaborate presentation you mailed out. It is just not a radio station. We are only interested in the music and whether or not it fits within the direction of our programming. That means all any program director would need from you is the single you have chosen to service radio. They do not need your poster, your 8x10, a list of who you sang with 10 years ago – just your single and contact information. Is that really all, Denise? Yes and no. Yes, that is the initial offering. No, because that initial offering must work in conjunction with additional aspects of the industry. Many of the additional aspects have been discussed in the marketing chapter and will continue to be discussed throughout this book.

Many independent recording artists are unwise with the breakdown of their budget, particularly as they learn to maneuver their way through their first project. Because of this, their focus is to press full projects and get those out. Review the chapter on marketing to understand why that is not productive to your branding goals. For your radio purposes, sending a full project to program directors works against your desire to get noticed and reviewed. Let me explain.

When program directors receive a crate full of envelopes from the mailroom they have to prioritize in order to efficiently perform all their duties as program director. I am aware of the perception among many label representatives that program directors have nothing else to do but listen to music and schedule it for airplay. Not so. Particularly if the station is in a major market, there is much work to do to establish your station and remain a competitive force against other gospel, secular, and mainstream stations in the market. Time to just sit and listen to 5-50 full projects per week is rare.

I once had a rep for Sony's gospel division get completely offended when I told him his CD was "in review." He replied, "How hard is it to listen to a CD? You just put it in your car CD player on your way home. It's not that hard." He was so disrespectful that I would normally dismiss any future submissions from him on the basis of his attitude. But I knew of the impending dismantling of Sony's gospel division, and that this particular rep and his opinion soon would have no further presence in this industry. Furthermore, arguing with someone whose perspective was limited would have been futile. He understood promoting but he never stood in the shoes of a program director to know that yes, just popping a CD in the car on your way home was too hard.

In this high-technology world program directors answer e-mails in the car, return calls, and continually listen to their station and their competitors'. Heaven help if there is to be any personal life where a child or spouse wants to hear their favorite music or if a PD just wants some time to relax and enjoy time for self. On the off chance a program or music director does take home CDs to review, how, among the many submitted, do they decide which ones to listen to? Prioritize.

The method most program directors use to prioritize is this: as projects come in they are opened, all extra materials are tossed and the CD project/single is stacked. The time the average major-market program director sets aside to review the music is once or twice a week, so each day as more projects come in, the stack increases until time to review. At that time the stack is divided into categories. This is where the visual packaging issues discussed in the previous chapter come into play. If you are an unknown artist or label it will be known quickly because the name on the project will be unfamiliar. Those core artists whose name and label are familiar begin a stack for immediate review. Yes, a never-heard-before Fred

Hammond single will be set aside to listen to immediately. On the contrary, "John Smith" will remain for further assessment as to whether it will make a review stack at all.

Once the artist and label name is determined unfamiliar, most program directors begin to analyze the project's visual cues. This is why you must be on point with your imaging and marketing. If I program a station that is contemporary-heavy and the artwork on your CD project features four guys in canary yellow suits with matching alligators, the perception is instantly quartet. Since I may not rotate much quartet, for example, that would be strike two for that project. First, it is an unfamiliar artist; second, it is likely not music that fits my programming. There is still nothing motivating the average program director to review your project or play it on their station. Is there a strike three? It is likely.

The third strike most independent artists unknowingly experience when seeking radio play is the failure to follow up. There is no one pushing the product on the phone, on the e-mail, in the market establishing a relationship with those who have influence over a listening, actively purchasing audience. There are well-established gospel radio promoters who will tell you even they, with 15 years of experience and industry relationships, will not see results of serviced product until they themselves get on the phone and personally ask a program directors for support of an artist. Neither their assistants nor another industry unknown would realize success. They, with the relationships, needed to follow up on behalf of their artist to find success.

One such case I remember was early 2008, just after the Stellar Awards. Maurette Brown Clark had walked away with two awards for her and her daughter. Her first live project was receiving good airplay and was in the top five on the charts. It was a very respectable place any artist would love to be. On one particular chart she seemed to be stuck at number two. Her label of the time, Malaco Records, is a major, established name in the industry but do not have equal resources in finances or personnel when compared to a mega-label like Verity Records

(Zomba Gospel). Weekly telephone tracking did not occur, though I would receive product and e-mail blasts regularly. Because of the familiarity of the label and the roster of artists, product never got tossed, but was reviewed and often added though personal contact with a representative was occasional. When it did occur I spoke with D.A. Johnson, who had established himself as a credible promoter and industry exec.

One day, as Stellar Award winner Maurette Brown Clark sat #2 on the charts with her hit "One God," I got a call. Lo and behold it was D.A. Johnson with whom I probably had not spoken since I left D.C. a couple years prior. It turns out Maurette was only some 18 spins away from achieving her first number one single. With some increased spins from a few major markets, "One God" would make history for Maurette. D.A. was on the line to personally ask for the support. New York loves Maurette Brown Clark. I, as the Program Director of WLIB in New York felt that hometown support (as she was originally from Long Island) would be appropriate. The song was hot, on the charts, highly requested, and already in heavy rotation. A few more spins over the weekend were perfectly justified. If, for example, I played it two to three more times over a 72-hour period, and five other stations played it three to five more times as well, Malaco would have met its goal and their artist, Maurette Brown Clark, would receive her first #1 single. They did and she did.

That next week "One God" by Maurette Brown Clark entered the #1 position on one of the industry's gospel music charts and the goal had been achieved. That milestone would have been completely missed had a credible person with professional relationships among program directors not reached out with a personal request. Very few, if any, program directors follow spins. Why? Because, in our arrogance we really do not care what another station in another market is doing, nor do we program spins to satisfy the sales or promotional goals of a label. We only care to the extent that it affects us, how it reflects on our playlist, or the progress of our programming. There would have been no way for me to know one of our hometown artists was so close unless the communication of the relationship was made.

This is precisely what many independent artists are lacking – professional relationships or access to someone with professional relationships to speak on their behalf. This is strike three. Strike One, you are an unfamiliar name. Strike Two, you are perceived as music that does not fit the programming. Strike Three, no personal follow-up or professional relationship and you're out. Literally, your CD is out the door with the street team or trash. That is harsh but real. On occasion I have personally given un-played product to shelters or college radio stations, or donated them to libraries, all of which are worthy causes but none of which help to achieve your goal of airplay.

So how can you, the independent gospel artist, find success in this process? You must understand a few realities then develop the best plan for you.

Someone must establish contact.

Imagine that you have no expectation of an individual or group coming to your home yet a stranger knocks on your door, enters with a bag full of extra stuff, and just stands in your living room. You find it odd yet do not call the police nor throw them out. A day passes, maybe two, and they are still standing there waiting on you. You are not sure who they are. You do not know anything about them. You have an interest to know more but can not act on it because of the duties you must fulfill around your home. The responsibility to the kids, the spouse, the cleaning, the cooking all pull you away from asking, "Who are you?" and they continue to just sit there volunteering no answers. A few more days pass and you need space for seating for the children you are familiar with and the spouse you love. Now, this stranger has got to go. They are put out having never revealed the treasure that is within them.

Perhaps an unrealistic example, but this is what an independent artist who does not communicate or who has no one representing them is like. Someone must make contact to establish a professional relationship and create awareness of the product. Preferably this should happen prior to a package hitting a program director's desk. A good consultant will tell you there should be pre-release promotion that includes this communication before or within close proximity of a single being received by a program director. When this does not occur, the package – music and all – is likely to be wasted. If and when communication is finally established, assuming there is interest, the request of you as the artist and label will be to re-service that same product, costing you additional money that could have been avoided with a simple phone call. As you will learn about rotation and space for airplay shortly, there also is limited space on one's desk. Your project is not going to sit there long before it is discarded one way or the other.

You must make contact and have a program director on alert, looking out for your project. As I said if you wait it will be trashed and you will have to send another when someone is paying attention, costing you more money. Furthermore, it is best for you to make the contact. I know in the previous chapters I speak about hiring an independent promoter who has established relationships with program directors and music directors. That suggestion is not a replacement for you making contact as well and establishing your own relationships.

Many parents at one time or another are caught in the dilemma of wanting to give a child care provider a piece of their mind. Why? Because they did or did not do something the way the parent thought should be done concerning their baby. It was definitely not the way they as the parents would have done it. But the reality is no one will take care of your child with as much love and concern as you will. Likewise, no one can push your passion or care for your creation as much as you. When it comes to describing the sound of your music, explaining the influences of your ministry, or expressing the willingness to pursue your passion, no one can verbalize that better than you because it comes from you. You are your own best representation.

"But I have no relationships in the industry, which is why I am paying a promoter." True, but understand that that promoter has established those relationships though years of promoting, networking, conferences, conventions, and connections. The most effective independent promoters have been in the industry for at least 15 years, and most will tell you their relationships did not begin to prove themselves until at least five years into doing it professionally. When I say, "prove themselves" I mean they did not reach a point of credibility and reputation where they could easily and effectively see results until five years of talking to, e-mailing, servicing, and connecting with the same industry folks. For you to reach that same level of credibility you must put in the time and effort to know those in the industry, as well as allow them to know you. That is what you should be working on while your hired promoter seeks airplay and exposure.

You should contact program directors just to introduce yourself. You are not seeking to track or undermine what you have spent money for someone else to do. You simply are seeking to make casual conversation for the purpose of establishing a relationship to further your stated goals. How much effort you put into this process will determine how long it takes for you to develop a professional presence in the industry.

If you still do not understand why you need to do this work for yourself, in addition to paying someone who already has established connections, let me offer another illustration to prove a more compelling point. I was hired around 2000 to consult and promote an independent holy hip-hop artist. We were doing well establishing a name and gaining exposure. By this time I had been on the radio in a major market for some time and had established a number of relationships with label executives, managers, fellow announcers, and program directors from across the nation. Through one such relationship, an opportunity presented itself for my client to share the stage with an established nationally-known holy hip-hop artist. Because of my relationship with the label rep the national artists were willing to perform at my artist's event at no charge. The label would foot the bill and I would guarantee promotion of the event and his artists' new single.

During the process of preparing this upcoming event, a challenge I was battling continued to persist. My client was bouncing checks and not paying me for my work. Finally the one time I needed a check of his to clear it, once again, bounced. What made it worse was his constant reassurance that "the money is there." My personal finances were affected as checks I wrote began to bounce due to his insufficient deposit. I was done. Remaining as professional as possible, I issued a formal letter terminating our agreement due to lack of payment. When I stopped working with this artist my connections stopped working for him. I let those with whom I was working on behalf of this artist know that I was no longer associated with the artist or his project. They were welcome to continue working with him on the upcoming event but no correspondence would be through me.

All the forward momentum completely stopped. Within a brief period of time retailers moved the project to the back of the shelf, then off the shelf as radio airplay came to a halt. Event promoters did not return his calls for a spot on their events, and most importantly the national artists scheduled to appear at his event backed out. When I told the record label rep that I was no longer associated with him but they could still do the event he said to me, "Denise I don't know him." When my former client made direct contact with the label rep to secure the artist there was now a $3,500-plus travel and hotel price tag attached.

When the person with the contacts leaves they leave with the contacts, and if you have not developed relationships for yourself you will be in a position where all progress stops and you will have to begin again, no matter how popular or successful you have become. Take the time and energy to get to know people personally.

Lastly, when attempting to build relationships it is best to do it during the times program and music directors have set aside to interact with you. You do not want to force yourself on a PD or make yourself a nuisance. Most who are in a charge of programming set aside "music days," also known as "tracking days." These are specific days and specific times set aside for labels and/or artists to pitch their music as well as track the progress of a specific single or artist.

Many will allow office visits during these times, but call first to confirm. If they do not allow it make sure you call within their specified time, being mindful of the time zone differences. If there is no progress on your single, make sure you ask about a good time to follow up on its status. The PD may have no intentions of considering it for a few weeks. Your calling each week will serve no purpose and the pressure you place may become detrimental to your new relationship.

You must be willing to invest in yourself.

It is obvious through the elaborate packages and studio expenses to produce a project, for example, that you are willing to spend money. What I am referring to in this point is not that you have to spend money but rather change your thinking from spending to investing in yourself. When you are just willing to spend money, you will purchase this and pay for that and waste away your resources chasing something. However, when you invest, you put conscious thought into how the money is utilized and make an effort to ensure that it is utilized in the most effective and efficient way to secure the best possible return.

Millionaires have the ability to purchase multiple properties. But when they actually do, they have researched how the property will in the near and/or distant future yield a return on the initial cost. If they chose to use the property as a residence they know prior to purchase if it is a desirable location, if there is historical value, and how it will perform in future markets. The same holds true if the millionaire chooses to utilize the property for a business or rental property. Thought and research goes into whether the return is worth the cost. Most independent artists have not researched enough prior to this book to know that the cost of a premium plastic folder for your package will not yield the desired return of airplay, yet Staples and Office Depot continue to reap the benefits of artists spending rather than investing.

Take the time to consciously determine if where you are about to spend your money is the place that will yield you the greatest return. Money is absolutely necessary for your success. That is the nature of this business, but considering that the source is your pocket, you must use wisdom when allocating funds. Please also understand, investing in yourself is not solely a monetary issue. You will need to offer your time as well and your energy.

Your time: we discussed in a previous chapter about the type of person you are, so the introspection concerning how you will balance artist and family time should be well underway. But what about your work? Most independent artists hold down full-time employment amidst trying to get a professional music career off the ground. Some of that nine-to-five time will have to be spent doing artist business, in this case contacting radio. Even if you hire someone to handle your business for you, believe me, you will spend daily nine-to-five time phoning them for updates and to ask and answer questions concerning your vision. The key is, just like when considering money, you weigh whether or not that telephone or e-mail time for your business and not for your nine-to-five is worth the return. I hear a passionate artist saying, "Everything I do for this is worth it." Breathe.

You are not just considering the value of the return but also if the resource is being spent effectively and efficiently. Your getting fired because you keep taking calls about non-nine-to-five business will not benefit anything. However, if the importance is weighed and things are prioritized, I am sure you will see additional options. For example, instead of wasting 20 minutes going out for lunch, bring lunch from home and never leave your desk. Utilize that time to make and return calls. I strongly suggest you view the Will Smith movie, *The Pursuit of Happiness.* Remember, he got ahead by being a good steward of his time. While others got up to get a drink, he never moved. He even saved seconds by never hanging up the phone. Every second, just like every dollar to an independent artist, is important. Make it count.

Furthermore, there are blueprints to this artist thing. Many have come before you and found success using many of the same promotional methods. Among them is the promotional tour. I have already illustrated how important it is for you to get yourself in front of industry professionals. Conventions and workshops rarely afford you the one-on-one time you need to develop a professional relationship. You need to get in front of them in their office and in front of their mic at their station. While in town you also need to get on someone's stage or in someone's pulpit to sing, rap, or play.

To ensure you have a one-to-two week stretch to work the region or nation you need to save your money and horde your vacation time. You should even consider asking your co-workers who believe in your ministry to donate some of their vacation time to you. Most human resource departments will allow that. A regional or national promotional tour to support your project is an investment, and a much better way to spend time and money than losing a day of work because you had to drive all over town signing comp deals with local Christian music and bookstores so you can say your CD is in a store. You can do that on a Saturday.

Do not convince yourself you are giving up your vacation time either. Map your route and schedule your daily activities to have the time to experience the sights and attractions of each city you visit. Bring the family and enjoy the vacation. You have a built in promotional team ready to pass out your handbills when not at the nearby Six Flags. And please do not forget to keep receipts to write off your business expenses. There is a way to make it happen. Research the wisest, most effective, and most efficient way to invest in you.

Make noise so others can hear.

If a tree falls in the forest and no one is there to hear, does it make a sound? If you release your CD in Jacksonville, Florida, and I am in New York, do I know? Though program directors from across the nation discuss music with each other, there are hundreds of established artists – not to mention the endless supply of indies – making the likelihood of your name being mentioned very slim. You must take it upon yourself as the label to inform the industry of you, your music, your ministry, and your activities. If I receive an e-blast with a list of eight tour dates and I see my market and a familiar location on that e-mail, I am likely to contact you not because you are the greatest artist, but because I, too, want to invest my time and the time and resources of my radio station wisely.

If you are making serious noise in a market without that local gospel station spinning you they will feel the pressure. Yes, you will benefit from the exposure the station will provide and will likely achieve your goal of airplay (though minimal); but the station, also, will continue its goal to establish itself to its listeners as the place connected to anything gospel and hot. You see, radio, gospel or not, is a business. Supporting you has got to make sense to it. A station that is connected to Fred Hammond ministering in town will reap benefits of exposure and branding. But you are not Fred Hammond. That does not mean you do not have to carry yourself and present yourself as though you are, however, and when I know you, an indie, have your name on the tongues of a number of my listeners, it is in my best interest to come on board.

E-blasts, flyers, commercial time, and other such repetition all help to puff up a program director's perception of you. Please, once again, make sure your efforts are the most effective. If you send an e-blast about your appearance in a three-day revival with Tye Tribbett in North Carolina to a program director in D.C. it does not pass the "Who cares?" test. Make it make sense for them and make it work for you.

It is not your right.

Many times the arrogance of independent artists is what aborts their success. Radio play is not your right. There is nothing that says any radio station, even your local one, must play your music. Get real. I am sure you are a blessing in your church, and that your mother loves your music. I even understand that you truly believe you can do better than many established national artists. And? That still does not make it your right to get spins on a commercial radio station. Even Kirk Franklin, in his multi-platinum-ness, after receiving the airplay you seek, is tested and his radio performance is constantly evaluated.

Money, ratings performance, and jobs are on the line at every gospel radio station across the nation. There is no power trip where program directors just want to keep the little guy out. This is a serious business with serious consequences to every action and decision. These consequences can cost companies a lot of money and those in radio a lot of jobs. It is nothing personal but strictly from a business perspective, no one – from you to the top gospel artist (or his/her music) – is worth sacrificing any of that. There is a big picture.

There is market research, focus groups, testing and re-testing to see what (and who) works and does not work. When advertising money is on the table and twenty stations of all formats are grabbing for it, stations strategically go for and stick with what is proven to work, and a proven hit is guaranteed to work every time over an unknown artist with an unknown song. James Cleveland's "God Is" is a proven hit that a PD will always get results with. Can the same be said for "Jesus is my Homie" by The Jesus Freaks? To my knowledge that is not a real group or a real song, but if they were and they were played today they would be as foreign to you on the radio as they are in this book.

That is why you have to learn and understand the process and thinking of radio programmers. It is so little about you and more about what will give this business the greatest numbers and the most money. However, there are select opportunities available to un-established artists, opportunities you will miss if you let frustration and arrogance enter your heart. Remember Christ, remain humble, and make your music, and you will be easy to support.

There is only so much space.

If a person can look at a clock and understand that each line represents a second or minute and there are only 60 seconds in each minute and 60 minutes in each hour, then they also should understand there are only so many songs one can rotate within a 24-hour period.

Without feeling like I am in college teaching radio again, let me give you a crash course in programming. There are four main categories of music you need to know. They are Power, Secondary Power, Recurrent, and New. Singles that get what most know as "regular rotation" fall into one of these categories. Powers or "A-songs" are your hottest songs by the top artists. These are the songs that you hear every three to five hours. In secular radio you may hear them every two hours. Most radio consultants agree you need 6-10 songs in this category, and there are typically two songs from this category in an hour. Likewise, your Secondary Powers or B songs are your second-hottest songs. Again, there are 6-10 songs in this category and two from this category within an hour. Your Recurrents were once powers but are declining in popularity. However, they are familiar to the audience and have been proven as hits. There may be twenty to thirty in this category and one to three within an hour. Your New songs are just that, relatively unfamiliar songs that you want to introduce to your audience. There are 6-10 songs in this category, though they do not have as many opportunities in an hour to get scheduled when compared to a Power, so they are not rotated as frequently. You usually hear at least one New song within an hour of programming.

Why did I go through that with you? Because, if you do the math, that amounts to approximately seven songs scheduled within one programmed hour with an average of 10 total songs per hour (classic and decade songs make up the difference). The same 30 songs from your A, B, and New categories make this trip hour after hour waiting for their turn to come around again. That cyclical wait is called a rotation. The songs rotate and to achieve the three to five hour repetition that research says the listeners want to achieve familiarity and for their favorite song to return to the airways, there cannot be a large volume of choices in the pot. The more songs in each category, the longer it takes to get a song around again.

That makes 30 songs, 50 if you include the Recurrent category, making their way in a rotation, hour after hour. If your song is number 51 on the desk of the program director you will not be added. No matter how great a Smokie Norful song is or how anointed a Kurt Carr song is, there is only so much space in a programmer's inventory. In 2008 Marvin Sapp's hit "Never Would Have Made It" broke the record for the song to stay at #1 the longest. Do you know how many established artists waited for him to begin a descent to make room for someone else? How much longer for you as an unknown indie assuming you have all other aspects covered?

While sales and rotation kept that particular single at #1, please understand that core artists are not exempt from being dropped from rotation. There are a few reasons a song by any artist may drop in rotation. One reason is if the relationship between the station and the artist/label fails. Some program directors will pull or blacklist a song or artist if station requests are not met at the expense of the label or if they are offended in some other way. Is that wrong? Yes. Does it happen? Absolutely.

Another reason a song may drop in rotation is if the artist and single are no longer priority at their label. Remember, if no one is representing you, keeping your music and name before the powers that be, you do not exist for that time in programming history. If a label, independent or major, does not have you as their priority, it will show in your airplay.

A third reason a song may drop in rotation is if there is decreased performance on the charts or on playlists throughout the country. Picking a song to rotate over another song requires some form of justification. Just because you ask for it is not good enough. Just because we like the artist, or the song really blesses us is not good enough. There must be some objective supporting evidence, if you will, for the decision to rotate a song.

The last reason a single may drop in rotation is also in the same realm of justification. If a single does not test well it will likely be dropped. This is the reason that program directors find it close to useless for a promoter to say, "We are getting spins in D.C., and Philly just added it, and it's doing well in Jacksonville..." For a Program Director in Atlanta, how a single is performing in another market does not interest. How are the listeners receiving it? How do listeners feel about it? That is where testing comes in. A sample of listeners from a specific market is gathered and for compensation they listen to snippets of pre-selected songs then rate their likeability and familiarity. Low rating songs are re-evaluated and often adjusted out of rotation. That does not mean it will never be played again. It will simply lose its primo spot among those 30 select. If you are fortunate enough to receive regular rotation in any market and you begin to decrease in spins, it will likely be due to one of the preceding reasons.

Because regular rotation spots are limited, I always encourage independent artists to ask about other options. Do not solely focus on the Power category. You may never get there. But it does not have to be "there or no where." Many programmers have specialty shows to address areas that are underserved in the gospel music community. For example, there may be a one-hour holy hip-hop show, or a late night inspirational jazz or gospel neo-soul show. Search the features of each personality's show as well. Usually you can find out on the station's web site or by asking the program director if there is a new artist or "up-and-coming" spotlight. Even if your song gets played during that one spotlight moment, that is one more spin than you had.

Also, gimmicks work. I am not referring to those cheesy manufactured gimmicks that you can see through before the manila bubble envelope with your single in it is opened. I am talking about the legitimate single that would work perfectly for Mother's Day or that "blood" and "He got up" song program directors always look for come Resurrection Sunday. Most importantly, I always suggest a Christmas single and the more original the better. I personally could do without another version of "Silent Night" but the industry is always in need of good original Christmas music. Really, by the time we get to December 24 we are rotating only holiday music. That is a lot of one specialized category of music and you can never have enough. The beauty of including a Christmas single on your project is that if it is a hit, program directors have to return to it (and to you) year after year after year. There may only be so much space but you can find alternate ways to be effective.

Not now does not mean never.

You learned this in the previous point about rotation. It takes time for songs to rotate out and make space for the addition of new songs. Many independent artists, or at least their money to pay a promoter, give up and out too soon. Wise counsel once told me it is precisely when you feel like giving up that your breakthrough is close. I have learned that it is so true. You work and work and work with a goal in mind and just when you feel as though it will never come and you may as well move on, your turn is right around the corner.

Please understand my little motivational thought is not a promise that if you keep pressing for radio airplay forever, eventually your song will get played. That is not what I am saying. The reality is, that bit of motivation is not for every artist reading this book. There are many that may never receive any airplay. There are many who just do not have the image the industry is looking to support, the music that is suitable for commercial consumption, and several who just are not pleasing to listen to. But for those who are that and more and are just pressing for that moment when purpose and the timing of God meet, know that it will eventually come.

When I began at WLIB in New York everything was beginning. The format was new, the personalities were new, and much of the music was new to a market that had not had a regular source of gospel in many decades. Many of the people, issues, events, etc., that were not vital to the immediate establishment and survival of all this newness were pushed to the side. Many of the tri-states' own independent artists fell victim to the circumstances as well.

I recall one particular artist sent his CD. Then he sent his CD again and I believe e-mailed as well. He had an opportunity to meet and sit with me at a station brunch and once again submitted a CD. He even asked for my personal consulting assistance. "Anything" was a word he used frequently to stress his passion for getting this out. At that time I just could not do it. My schedule and attention were very strained and moreover, he was not a core artist and was not on the radar at all. There was no disrespect or malice intended but he was just not a priority. The CDs faded to the background before disappearing completely.

Fast forward a year later. I received a call from an independent radio promoter. C. Barry Martin is a credible promoter who listens to the music of the artists he promotes. So when he is pitching an artist or single he can speak personally on it and help a programmer visualize where it could have the potential to fit in your programming. When C. Barry got a hold of me I had not spoken to him on the phone in a couple of years. We usually communicated via e-mail but this time he called and got me on the first ring. At the end of his list of artists he was tracking he mentioned one last artist. "I know that name," I said to him. I begin to describe the CD cover to him and sure enough, it was that same artist who I simply hadn't had time to review just a year ago. The difference now was not just the fact he had a credible person with a relationship speaking for him, but also that this call came almost two years after the launch of the station. Our station's lineup had settled, ratings were good, folks were breathing easier and had a routine down. That routine included space to explore more music that would accent programming features.

Of course we have our regularly rotated songs but there was space to accent some elements within individual day parts. C. Barry was happy I was familiar with this gentleman, though I had to admit I was not familiar with his music. He asked about any worship programming. Lo and behold there were multiple times throughout the week where personalities prayed. He sent me to a specific single and promised it would serve the atmosphere we were attempting to create. This time when I got the project, I knew exactly what to look for and went right to the single; it delivered and one year later the artist got his airplay.

Be patient. If a programmer does not have the space or creative programming opportunity to play your single now, it does not mean space will never become available. Everyone in the various areas of this industry has a goal they are trying to meet. Your song may not fit a programmer's plan right now. It took the Samaritan woman three times for Jesus to subtly point Himself out to her as the one she sought before He had to straight up tell her, "I am He," and she got what she was looking for. Time is not your enemy. Do not despise it. The truth about the participation radio needs to have in your music ministry will become as clear as the Messiah. It may just take a few times.

If, after reviewing these realities of radio you realize you still have little to no clue how to develop a radio promotions plan as part of your marketing strategy, hire a reputable consultant to develop one for you. Do not forget, the written strategy will typically cost you one fee. If offered, spend the extra money for regular access to the consultant so they can help guide and advise you through the process.

Part III

PROFITING

Chapter 8

THE BUSINESS OF IT ALL

MAKING MONEY

There are a multitude of avenues open to artists for their financial support. Some are obvious and others are non-traditional. I have always held that as an independent artist, your money will go as far as your creativity will allow it. There are ideas yet to be explored. There are methods yet to be implemented. Performances, preaching, endorsements, sponsorships, writing, voice-overs, soundtracks, programming material, teaching, consulting, downloads, ring tones, etc., etc., – there is no way for me to offer you every possible method of making money in this industry. There are just too many, and many that have yet to be discovered. However, I would like to offer some information for you to consider.

The two traditional ways artists make money is through product and performances. We discussed in the chapter on marketing the issue of pricing. In my experience I have found that the average freshman gospel artist proceeds with complete uncertainty. The first hurdle they have to tackle is the discomfort of placing a price on what is for Christ. We will discuss this challenge in this chapter's section titled, "Ministry vs. Industry." Once the hurdle is cleared and an artist chooses to charge for their services, they enter with great caution, requesting only a few dollars or a "love offering" for their time and efforts. Many will come for free if they are able to sell product.

Please do not view my words as a condemnation of this process. To the contrary, I am acknowledging what I have experienced first through many years of being an artist, then throughout many years of working with artists and their personal distress in this area.

I cannot give you a reference chart to use when questions arise as to what to charge. There are too many variables. Many have been discussed throughout this book, including balance in your home, the value of your time, your ability to draw an audience, and more. What I can tell you is to beware of overcharging and undercharging. They both have implications.

Remember when you were a kid and you pleaded for that box of cereal with the prize inside? It was the Joe action figure you had to have, yet while enthralled with the tiny picture of your treasure on the box your immature eye did not see the small print that read, "Actual Size." You get home, tear the box open and begin digging into mounds of sugary goodness for the small plastic bag peeking underneath. At last – your action figure that is…..1 inch tall. Even mom is disappointed she paid for something so small.

When the quality and expectation does not equal the compensation, you are overcharging. Your integrity will deem whether you proceed in that direction. But understand this: no one should ever leave one of your performances thinking, "That was not worth it." You should not leave a negotiation or business/performance deal feeling devalued either. You have to know and understand your worth lest you be exploited. Yes there are promoters and Christians that will try to benefit from your desire to minister and perform. Where the exchange is mutually beneficial is when it should be deemed worth it.

However, if your services have been requested and you have been sought out to appear and perform, that promoter or ministry sees value in your presence. If there is a budget and a minimum they are compensating others, you have a right to expect at least that. Do not be afraid to ask what their budget is for an artist. That will give you a point of reference. Should you choose to negotiate greater is your option, but requesting just a love offering or product table is undervaluing yourself and what is offered through you.

Within the most passionate independent gospel artists wars the continual battle in mastering balance. We discussed having a well-conceived marketing strategy to help focus and organize you. Unfortunately there is also a battle between staying focused and feeding your passion. Be careful not to allow yourself to get caught up in saying yes to every performance request. Every opportunity will not benefit your career and spiritually, you are not assigned to be used in every situation. I have heard artists on the verge of burnout justify their schedules by saying "God gave me this gift and if I don't use it He'll take it away." That statement is only half true.

He did give you your talent. However, it is not about the amount of use. It is about stewardship. He has called you to be a good steward over your talent. In Mathew 25 the kingdom of God is compared to the actions of servants who were given talents. No particular instructions were given these servants, but through their discernment, creativity, and efforts two of them found a way to be a blessing and become prosperous through what had been given them. In different ways they doubled what they were given and because they found a way to prove profitable with the little they were given, the master knew they could be trusted with greater.

If this is to be compared to the kingdom of God, as the Word says, then one interpretation is that the responsibility of ministry given these servants was to result in new souls, for example. Though they approached the task differently they focused, organized, and executed according to the purpose of their master. He never wanted them to be unproductive. What master wants an unproductive servant? Imagine if they ran here and there throughout the countryside getting half a talent from this person then a quarter from that person then one from another – how unprofitable and ineffective would they have been when the master returned?

Likewise, running yourself into the ground to sell ten CDs here, eight there, and twelve over there until you are fatigued, frustrated, and unproductive is not good. Furthermore you become unusable for future ministry opportunities He (the Master) has prepared and assigned you to. You become ineffective and unprofitable for the kingdom not to mention your career.

As for the one in the scripture with the one talent, please do not get caught up in contrasting yourself with him and pointing out that you are not hiding your talent but rather using it. The point of the parable is that he was unprofitable. The servant was set up to work for the kingdom and given a tool in the talents, expected to yield results. Whether you use your talents or hide them is irrelevant if in the end you still bear no fruit and are cast into a place where there is weeping and gnashing of teeth (also known as disappointment and frustration). Once again you must have focus, organization, and creativity, and when considering areas of business and money, discernment is vital.

MANAGEMENT

I always have found it interesting to hear an independent unknown artist refer to their manager. The immediate question in my head is 'what are they managing?' That thought is not to belittle the artist's self perception or their ongoing professional efforts. I have spoken on many occasions in this book about the need for a team or specifically individuals to assist in successfully achieving your goals. But a quality manager is almost something an artist must earn. Let me explain.

Most independent gospel artists are unknown and do not have enough industry or consumer impact (or potential impact) to attract the interest of a proven veteran manager. By default the bulk of the independent gospel artists of today have managers that are also unknown and attempting to make a name for themselves as well.

They do not have industry relationships outside of their immediate market, do not understand the basics of business and product promotion, do not know or speak the terminology of the industry, and lack other traits displayed by a seasoned successful artist's manager. It becomes a case of the blind leading the blind. Though well-intentioned I was one of those blind leading early in my career, so I speak from experience. An artist positions himself for disappointment when they sign a contract with a novice manager. The expectation of the artist is that the manager will make their name and their music known, that they will get the artist paid performances, and essentially they will manager like old-school Russell Simmons making things happen for Run DMC. It would do you good to read Russell Simmons autobiography, *Life and Def,* before you decide that is the struggle you want to take.

You will be contractually obligated to pay a manager a percentage of each performance and often times a portion of your publishing. Before you decide to pay someone for their on-the-job training you should re-read this book and feel empowered to manage yourself or at least keep it within the family. It will prove a greater benefit to you in the future. Eventually you will have more than you can handle and will feel the press of that next level. That is when God will place the right person in your path to handle and excel at those duties. Perhaps you will become so proficient at the business of the industry that you will never utilize a manager. Rather you will have a booking agent to deal with the logistics of engagement requests and an attorney to handle contracts. Vicki Winans developed a blueprint for artists to follow, proving success was still highly probable without a manager.

Perhaps it is the cheap in me. Perhaps it is the control freak. Experience, however, has fostered my belief that independent artists learn faster, grow professionally at an accelerated rate, have a better understanding of themselves as artists, and are able to personally establish the much-needed industry relationships when they are working for themselves. The stakes are higher. There is no one else to blame when things go wrong and no one else to claim the reward when the Father says, "Well done." Furthermore, when it is time for you to add others to your team you will know what to expect and the needed level of performance to ensure success because you have already set the standard.

The number-one reason independent artists feel a need to acquire a manager is to have someone responsible for keeping their calendar full. Should you choose to manage yourself here are some tips on getting and staying booked.

1. **Start at home.** Your home church has events that you perhaps brushed off as just your church's women's day or usher board anniversary event. That is an opportunity. And if you consider the visitors that come to see their co-worker or the family member that comes to witness their cousin's participation, you will see the potential for future opportunities as well. Participate in every non-Sunday morning service event available to you. They are opportunities for your music ministry to be seen as well as occasions for you to hone your skills.

2. **Ask around.** You have friends and family members that attend other churches in and out of the area. Inquire about their churches' upcoming events. If they are willing to approach the event organizer on your behalf let them. If they are not or you are uncertain about how you will be represented, ask them for the contact information of the president or organizer of the sponsoring auxiliary and offer your services yourself.

3. **Read.** Newspapers, magazines, and web sites have a barrage of information concerning upcoming events within your market and nationwide. By the time they reach the paper as

an advertisement the event may be completely booked. If not, great. Offer your services. If so, inquire as to the frequency of the event, establish a relationship, and plan on being a part of the next one. Contact persons for civic organizations, municipal centers, and park services can change frequently. Maintain relationship so you can be within immediate consideration of any replacement individual.

4. **Understand the calendar.** I repeat this sentiment within this book. You can take advantage of the calendar year if you prepare appropriately. Community organizations will always prepare King Day events. Black History Month is still every February. Churches, schools, colleges, and community organizations set aside funds for events each year. Look outside of your comfort zone of the black church. Other ethnicities like and appreciate African-American music and love to display it. At the beginning of every week is a Sunday, and in every affluent community there is a Sunday brunch at the local coffee house or jazz club where the patrons want to hear a soul-stirring version of "Amazing Grace," or "Do Lord." Who do you think continued to propel the music of The Blind Boys of Alabama 50-plus years into their career? Not the Black church. Next up on the calendar is Good Friday and Resurrection Sunday and on and on and on all the way to Christmas and Watch Night service. Understand the calendar and work it to your advantage.

5. **Have a brief but effective presentation package.** You will need one should someone request it or show interest in utilizing your

services. In the chapter on marketing we spoke about overselling yourself. People have a lot going on and a package-full of your materials and articles and reviews and such is too much to go through, especially when you are soliciting an organizer outside the Christian community, and especially if that much was not requested. There are creative ways to express and sell who you are in a concise manner. Consider a colorful pictured brochure with a mini-CD attached containing samples of your music or a DVD specifically produced and developed as a promotional tool to show performances and audience interaction to event organizers and concert promoters.

Please be realistic in seeking performance and ministry opportunities. There are event organizers who do not care if you have a project or are nationally known. If you can fulfill their event needs they are satisfied. However, attempting to get the opening act position at the sold-out Kirk Franklin concert when you have no hit song and no following is a bit unrealistic. The above are a few tips to help you get started. After that, relationship and referrals will keep the ball rolling. When it begins to roll out of your control solicit help in a booking agent or manager. Until then, you are your own best manager.

MINISTRY VERSUS INDUSTRY

I have heard many artists stress this career as a ministry once they achieve the success of a nationally recognized artist. It was not a sentiment stressed publicly in the beginning when they were on the grind trying to make their ministry pay their rent. What is most disheartening is when they go so far as to condemn upcoming artists for what they perceive to be industry work over ministry.

Though gospel music has consistently sold when other genres posted a decrease in sales, the sales of gospel music overall is still less than that of other formats. Even our counterparts in Christian music yield greater financial success than your average gospel artist. Logic would say the vast majority are in gospel music because they feel they have a basic call to spread the gospel of Christ through song. Do many get caught up in the quest for money and fame, forgetting some kingdom principles? Yes, and it is for that reason I offer this segment.

What are clearly considered "Industry" are those areas and aspects of your career that are entertainment-based, concern money, or deal with the promotion of your name, image, or associated products. That which is "Ministry" is anything directly attached to meeting a need for the glory of Christ and the message of His death, burial, resurrection, and ascension. It is just that plain and simple.

The gray areas come when we try to meld the two and justify what is done for us as a work for the kingdom. You cannot say that your commercial music career is purely ministry. That is impossible. Your commercial music ministry aspires to gain the acceptance of man through concert ticket and CD sales. If it did not you would simply have music dedicated to the message of Christ on a plain CD with no artist name, label logo, or web site address. If the name of Christ were the only name of concern in your efforts, there would be no mention of your name on a flyer or in a radio spot. A generic advertisement stating, "The gospel sung here," would be all it took.

The reality is that there is industry and there is ministry, and there is a business to them both. Let us operate in honesty rather than self-righteousness, and the wisdom allowing us to understand how to function successfully and effectively in the industry and for the kingdom will be revealed. The Father showed us by example the need for this understanding. He was a product of His industry and He had a ministry. Jesus also had a team.

While He focused on meeting needs (the definition of ministry), one disciple held the money, another one often spread the word of Jesus' coming as a promoter would, another met any personal needs as an assistant, and so forth. Perhaps there was a greater method to His choosing and compelling the particular men that became His disciples to follow Him. That was His team, similar to the one I, in previous chapters of this book, have suggested you develop. Each disciple had a business role to play to ensure the completion and success of the ministry.

His particular industry was the church or the kingdom of God. Jesus and His team proved to be the rebels of their industry by not operating within its set rules. The business side of the industry of church was clearly displayed through the political posturing and strategizing of the religious elite to orchestrate Jesus' death. That was business by those in the church. Fortunately, for our salvation the business of industry met pure ministry that Good Friday.

When you are launching a national ministry with many facets you do need a team to help you focus clearly on your ministry responsibilities. I asked J. Moss about this very issue. He is a businessman with PAJAM, negotiating contracts to originate songs and production for international secular superstars. However, when it came to J. Moss the gospel artist, I asked him how he does it all. He clearly and directly said, "You can't." He proceeded to explain that an artist cannot focus solely and completely on delivering the gospel of Christ through song while thinking of contracts and money and promotions. "That's why I have Walter," he said. Walter was his manager and focused on any business dealings, which freed J. Moss up to stay ever in the presence of God concerning the ministry He entrusted him with. From something as simple as scheduling an interview to an elaborate full band performance, Walter was the business.

As an independent artist you are not afforded the luxury of being available to focus so directly on ministry and ministry alone, and I would not advise it. If you leave the building of your house to another the foundation may not be sure. Keep pressing and that time will come.

I have witnessed new artists agonize over the decision of whether or not to ask for money to minister or perform. I sought to help by seeking to answer the question, how did Jesus get paid? How did he make money? He had a successful ministry by any generation's standards. It would be naive to believe He functioned in a natural state completely on the Spirit. To be images of Him in the Earth we should strive to be examples of Him in all areas, including ministry finances, but how? In my research and counsel with pastors and bible scholars the only supported conclusion I found was that the church, or those benefiting from being ministered to, provided for the minister, in this case Jesus and the disciples.

The provision may have been shelter for the extent of their stay in a particular city, fabric for garments, food for their journey, or money. But there was a tangible value seen in the kingdom efforts and actions of The Christ and He was compensated as a result. Through today's eyes we see the parallel in the form of honorariums and product sales. Unfortunately integrity is too often compromised in the industry and in the church causing a need for a more structured method. Without it most would prefer to utilize an artist's gift, while offering only the provision of gratitude.

This same "ministry versus industry" discussion can extend to performances as well. The question of whether Christians "gig" is often posed to me. I heard one platinum-selling gospel artist blast ministers of the gospel who use the term "gig" dictating that "gigging" is a secular method of performing and gospel artists minister. In my opinion it was quite a grand view and an easy perspective for a platinum-selling multi-millionaire to express. However, for the independent gospel artist who is never sure where the next love offering is coming from, "a gig" is a reality. The difference is a matter of the heart.

A gig is simply a performance date for money. There will be times when you take a date because you need the money.

Dipping into the household finances for the kingdom-building of your music ministry has taken its toll, and your gift to sing will need to be utilized like a skill or trade for money. Because you are a child of God you want someone to be touched and lives to be changed by the music you present, but in your heart you need the money. That is a gig.

You can and will do performances that are pure ministry whether the check does not clear or is non-existent. You just want God to be glorified, His anointing to fall, and souls to be saved. Just to be used by Him is an honor that never needs provision. In fact, if you never sing a lyric or play a note you would be content with simply being in His presence among the fellowship of the saints and those seeking to know Him more. That is ministry.

There is room in your life and career for both, much like your life accommodates a secular full-time job (an industry) and your gospel musical endeavors (ministry). Beware of those who are not in this entertainment industry, and who have not prayed with you concerning your purpose that try to place standards on you according to their understanding. During your professional commercial efforts you will hear, "be separate," and, "do not conform but be transformed," and much more used to justify others' beliefs about how your business and ministry should operate. Yes, your standards on how you present yourself and the integrity you operate in should exist at a higher standard than does those who have not found Christ. However, those standards will still have to function within the confines of this world system of commerce.

While I believe and stand by everything I have written in this segment, when it comes to ministry and the understanding of kingdom principles I strongly urge you seek the Father for the understanding you require for His purpose. This is my understanding that, according to His purpose through me, I have shared with you.

Chapter 9

YOU STILL WANT TO BE SIGNED?

After reaching the end of this book perhaps you are full on information. Maybe you are feeling empowered like you finally can see how to do this yourself and get results. Or perhaps you have always had a dream of being a signed artist and have only been selling out of your trunk because that big contract has yet to come through. Well, if you still think that down the line you may want to be signed, let me tell you some inside information no major label will tell you, before you take the publicity photo of you smiling next to all the label executives. The truth is you are smiling from the expectations and they are to. They expect you to make them money.

YOU ARE AN EMPLOYEE

A signed recording artist is contracted to work for a record label. Just like your employer hired you to work for them to do a particular job for the financial gain of the company, likewise a signed recording artist is employed to do a particular job (sing, rap, entertain) for the label it has signed with. Your personal wealth is not an issue to a record label. If you have to pay your mother's medical bills that is not their concern. Your inability to pay your rent is your own personal issue to deal with and not your employer's problem, not the label's. From your income you take your money and pay your mother's medical bills. You take your check and pay your rent. The problem is that as a signed artist you will get very few checks.

FAME DOES NOT EQUAL MONEY

"Tell them fame does not equal money," was an appropriate quote I heard from one Grammy award-winning gospel artist when I told him I was writing this book. Pastor Hezekiah Walker, who wrote the forward for this book, shared with me a testimony of his trials as a nationally known signed artist. Through basic industry practices he has been with multiple labels. One went under, another was purchased and his contract passed on and on again until settling with the largest gospel label and music conglomerate to date: Verity/Zomba Gospel. If the truth be told he was fortunate in the fact that many artists lose their contracts when labels are bought and sold. Being dropped from a roster, or fired, is not a good feeling.

But that was not his testimony. Instead his name and his music became known around the world. His choir songs became material for local church choirs to mimic and the appearance of his ministry became something for other recording choirs to aspire to. Unfortunately the appearance was greater than the reality.

Without going into great detail this world legend of gospel music did not receive a check until almost eight years into his professional career, and even then it was a publishing contract with a secondary company and not a check reflecting the revenue he generated for his label. While the entire nation and even my high school gospel choir were belting out "Clean Inside," he often found it difficult to maintain minimal, stable housing for his wife and child. Fortunately, after many, many years Pastor Walker was able to reconcile the financial differences with his label. Many artists who elevate to the status of a recognizable name and image eventually are able to profit from their efforts. Unfortunately, that category consists of an elite few in the industry.

Whether I am teaching a college course, or just a one-day seminar, one reality I try to instill is that the person you see is the last to get paid. The one in front of the camera, on the video, or on the microphone is the last to get paid in entertainment. When you hear of these multimillion-dollar deals, the person or company paying out is making four times off the talent than what they are paying. The tough thing for the artist or entertainer is that they have to maintain the image of being who the public believes them to be while in the midst of their reality of lack. It can be a very lonely place.

Not that I am a Grammy-winning, platinum-selling artist but I have lived this reality. I was the host of two popular radio shows (one national), talking to two million people daily, with a growing name in the industry. Even within my own family the perception was that financially, I was at least comfortable. The reality was far from it. I was in a one-bedroom apartment with my daughter and un-welcomed pests, living on borrowed furniture, while working any extra gig I could for some money. There was one point in my career I could not find full-time employment for five years and worked four part-time jobs. My own mother could not comprehend the fact that I made less in a year than her public school teaching salary was. Yet when I show up to host the hottest conference in town or stand next to someone's favorite gospel artist for a photo-op, no one wants to know, nor cares about, the reality. The perception of who you are is made greater than the truth.

This image that the signed artist is taken care of and can finally focus on music full time is a ruse. It is theater of the mind, smoke and mirrors, perpetuated by the industry itself through the display of the rented cars and mansions and award show performances — which, by the way, come out of a signed artist's budget as well. The way something looks is not always the way it is, and fame or popularity does not always equate to financial gain, particularly as a signed recording artist. Perhaps selling CDs does?

PLATINUM DOES NOT MEAN PAID

Let me do the math for you. Platinum means one million units sold. The average signed artist will make maybe $0.20 per unit sold. That is $200,000. A fortunate secular artist may make that amount in one year. Sounds good? Let's continue. Most major labels purchase units to inflate numbers and drive consumer demand. Therefore the accurate number sold may be more like 800,000. On top of not actually selling one million, the number of units purchased by the label for "promotional purposes" are charged back to you, the artist, as recoupable expenses (along with recording costs, video expenses, promotional travel expenses, any advance monies, and additional label expenses). Now your $200,000, the salary of a middle-level manager in New York City, is sizably cut. Oh, but we are not done yet.

If there is anything remaining from your income earned solely from product sales as a signed artist, you still will need to pay your lawyer, manager, assistant, and whomever else you choose to employ while still paying your monthly living expenses. At the end of the day you may have little to nothing to show for your globe-trotting appearances, world-renowned music, and recognizable face. And you will repeat this outcome for the length of your contract perhaps even compiling debt to the label as the balance from each project is added to the budget of the next.

The reality for the average signed gospel artist is that they will sell 80,000-300,000 units. The higher end is a good run to most gospel CDs. Those are considered your "A-list" gospel artists. As we continue in the age of downloads and other technological advances, that number of artists and units sold continue to dwindle. Though gospel remains the strongest CD-selling format, it still must adjust to the ever-changing consumer times. What does that mean for the signed artist? Not much, since most do not know before signing to negotiate download money, compilation income, or cross-medium usage of music.

If your label is releasing the soundtrack of a movie and a song you sing has been chosen for the project you get nothing for it. The same holds true should the label decide to release a "greatest hits" project or a compilation as in the very popular "WOW" series. That is additional money for the label. It was another way for them to make money with their product: you. And if you had no hand in the writing and your permission for publishing is not required, you may never know until the soundtrack is released that your name, image, and music were utilized.

There are two things to learn from this. First, you are a product or better yet, property. You are the property of the label. Your name, image, and music belong to them to utilize for the profit of the company. There was a period in music history where the artist Prince had the world "slave" written across his face. It was a protest to the practices of record labels that keep their artists bound and in poverty. His name was the property of the label (hence the brief change to a symbol), his image belonged to them, and they owned the rights to his music, forever. Prince fared well financially because he could demand $1 million for a performance and because he wrote his own music. That brings me to my second point. If you do not have publishing, you have nothing to accompany that platinum plaque.

YOUR OPINION DOES NOT MATTER

I believe I have beaten the property point into your understanding by now. But perhaps there is a basin of hope concerning your position when you choose to contract or sign with a recording company. I find that basin is filled with confusion over the phrase "artistic freedom." Maybe you understand and accept everything I have laid out thus far, but ascribe it to the business portion of the industry solely and not to the creative. What you must understand is that the creative through the artist is the product for the business. Just as any product goes through inspectors and managers for approval before hitting the consumer market, and is tested and re-tested for effectiveness while in the consumer market, so are you tested as the product.

Perhaps by your third, fourth, or fifth proven project you may have earned the right with your label to tell them the direction you want to go and lead the way. If that occurs you are in a fortunate place where you have established yourself as a money-maker for them. If you are a writer and musician you can simply submit the songs you have written. If you do not write you can choose to work with the producers and writers you desire then submit your work. However, after you have submitted the required 15-30 songs, the label will still dictate the final project. They approve the 12 tracks that will appear on a packaged project. Not you.

If you are a new artist, especially if you are not a writer or musician, rarely will you be given the opportunity to "screw up" the label's initial investment. They take few chances. The road map is laid out for you to follow and the larger the label, the more this holds true. This is a difficult transition particularly for artists who have grinded on their own terms for their own money for so long. Once you let go of your independence you sacrifice a lot. If you maintain yourself as a label yet sign an agreement with a parent company, you are still subject to them as any child would be to a parent.

Much of this sounds harsh and unbelievable to the starry-eyed artist who has the dream of being the next music icon and buying their mother a house with their first check. Believe it. The television series "Making the Band" was a wonderful depiction for those truly seeking an inside look into the industry. Of course the creators were careful to capture the entertainment aspect to benefit ratings but the critical eyes could see first hand the focus, structure, and control that exist within a label. There are people hired and assigned to develop and present every aspect of a product (you and your CD) in the most effective and profitable light for the company. There are those for your hair, wardrobe, posture, presentation, interview skills, choreography, vocal development, performance training, print campaigns, television campaigns, promotional tours, and on and on. At the end of it all it matters not if you agree with any of it.

Personally it was very sobering for me to hear the artist once known as Vanilla Ice, speak to this issue. Now sporting urban rocker flare, full of piercings and tattoos, he spoke about how the puffy pants and shiny suits he wore at his peak were never his taste or idea. With the phenomenon that was MC Hammer at the time receiving a very lucrative response with such an image, it seemed profitable for the label to take its product, the artist Vanilla Ice, in that direction. They did and made a fortune off his efforts. Unable to re-invent himself and with the label moving on to the next profitable concept for the industry, Vanilla Ice's music career would never exist on that level again. That was not his choice. He had no control and no opinion. That is a signed artist.

Vanilla Ice never wanted to be promoted as the white MC Hammer. He never wanted to be known as a white rapper, only a rapper. Unfortunately when you are a signed artist it does not matter how you choose to be promoted. There are, again, hired professionals that will research and give a strategy on the most effective and profitable way for you, the product, to be developed and promoted. If the label wants to promote you as "sexy and saved" and those hired can present how that image will be most effective, believe me, that will be what you come to be known as. This is so, whether or not you argue that the "singing single mom" would come across better to the church. Depending on your label and their vision for you, the church may not be your target audience.

Another issue to consider is the frustration of many signed artists with the extent of their promotion by their label. Though your label will bill you for whatever they spend on you, there is still a budget in place for exactly how much they are actually willing to spend on you. For artists that take off pretty fast more resources will be allocated to support the label's effort.

This is again at the artist's expense as well as at the expense of other artists. How? A label with a roster of 10 artists must focus on those that are performing to the benefit of the label.

The catch-22 dialogue between many artists and their label is, "Your CD is not performing well so it is not a promotional priority," from the label and, "How can my CD perform if you won't promote me?" from the artist. Signed artists who do not know to employ their own PR team are stuck with the one the label assigns who, unfortunately, has the label's goals as priority and not the artist's.

To get an artist's firsthand perspective on the issue of being signed versus independent I asked one of gospel's top independent artists what she thought were the benefits of being an independent artist over a signed label artist. A Christian hit-maker on both secular jazz charts and gospel music charts, Angella Christie, known as "The Barefoot Saxtress" had this response.

"There are many benefits but one must work hard and wisely to make the venture worth the while. It's no walk in the park, however, if music ministry is truly your calling, God will give you the grace and stamina to fulfill what has been required of you.

Benefits:

1. Owning your self.

2. Owning your own catalogue.

3. Creative Control. One has the freedom to choose the who, what, when, where and how of his recording process. Who will produce, play, or sing on the project. What songs will be recorded to be included on the final cut of the project. When and where the project will be recorded. How it will be recorded: whether live, studio or perhaps both.

4. Budget Control. Independent artists with knowing the right people can get a recording done more economically than a major label that spends heftily. This can allow you to see a return on your investment sooner.

5. The satisfaction of reaping a financial reward from the sale of your first CD purchased by a supporter – even though the recouping of expenditures must take place before it can be called a profit.

This is not for the faint hearted. It requires a great deal of maturity and organizational thinking. A good team will also be extremely important in the undertaking. Depending on the mindset of the individual this can be a lot of fun, although challenging. The challenge for most is not getting the final product in one's hands, but what to do afterwards."

These words from Angella Christie on the benefits of your status as an independent artist are wise and rooted in years of experience. They are also sentiments echoed by successful independent gospel artists throughout the industry. It would be irresponsible, however, to give you only this perspective of being signed. Becoming a signed artist indeed does have its benefits as well. You have access to areas of the industry because of the prestige and relationship of your label. Your exposure is heightened nationwide, and in many cases internationally. You also have the possibility of greater opportunities in the entertainment industry at large that would not be afforded the unknown artist. Lastly, all of this is at the expense of others. While you are obligated to pay back any monies spent on your behalf, you are not responsible for any upfront out-of-pocket costs.

There is a give and take in everything. There are pros and cons, benefits and liabilities in every decision you will be faced with throughout your career, signed or independent. With all the cheering I do for the indie artist to achieve and produce despite the odds of the industry and the monopoly of the majors, the truth is, as the success grows so does the inevitable transformation into the very image of the majors that indie artists rebel against. Consider the independent artist who gains national exposure and starts his own label, signs him/herself, then pulls up others that also were in the music struggle, contracting them as artists, eventually developing a roster needing national distribution and nationwide sustained promotion, etc., etc., which all blur the line of true independence. It becomes a matter of semantics and an irrelevant debate to participate in.

The point is to have the information needed to proceed toward the successful completion of a stated and written goal for your music ministry. None of the information in this segment, chapter, or book is meant to discourage you from your goals or what you believe God has called you to. Lack of knowledge can destroy. It can destroy dreams, devastate esteem, paralyze ministries, and cause you to question your very purpose in Christ. The enemy cannot take from you what God has prepared for and promised to you. However, he can get you to forfeit it. He does that through everyday situations and circumstances in life, business, and ministry. Prayerfully through the information presented here less space will be given to the enemy, and greater glory to the Father through your success.

GLOSSARY OF TERMS

Advertising – is a form of communication whose purpose is to inform potential customers about products and services and how to obtain and use them. Every major medium is used to deliver these messages, including: television, radio, movies, magazines, newspapers, video games, the Internet, and billboards. Marketers place advertising under the promotion segment of an overall Marketing Plan.

Arbitron – A radio audience research and measurement firm

Branding – Branding allows a company to differentiate themselves from the competition and, in the process, to bond with their customers to create loyalty.

Consignment – This is a percentage agreement you have worked out with individual retail outlets. The retailer will typically allow you to set the retail price but the percentage will not change. If it is 60-40 they will receive 60% of what the CD sells for whether you set the price at $10 or $15.99.

Core artist – A core artist is an established and relevant artist with proven hits. They have songs an audience is guaranteed to love so you will find them in a station's rotation.

In review – When a program or music director says your project is "in review," they mean it is in a holding state. They have either not listened to it yet but plan to or they have listened and have not made a decision as to whether it will be added or not. It is better to receive an "in review" than a no.

Independent Promoter – This is a music promoter who is not exclusively contracted or employed by a label. They are self-employed and have the flexibility to work with any artist and any project.

Indie – This is an independent gospel artist. It is also a term many retailers and media professionals will use to categorize underground or non-mainstream aritists, particularly of alternative genres.

Industry Relations (similar to PRMarketing) – This is the continual process of planning and executing the marketing mix (Product, Price, Placement, Promotion) of products, services, or ideas to create exchange between individuals and organizations. Marketing is also concerned with anticipating the customers' future needs and wants, which are often discovered through market research. Essentially, marketing is the process of creating or directing a business or organization to be successful in selling a product or service that people not only desire, but are willing to buy.

Music day – This is the day and time each week a program director or music director sets aside to track with label reps. Most will track over the phone but in many cases there are opportunities to personally meet on a first–come, first-served basis. If they only meet with five people, then you must be one of the first five to sign in, or you will not be seen.

Music Director (MD) – Employee of a radio station responsible for maintaining music logs and playlists, as well as tracking and keeping correspondence with record labels and artists.

P & D – Promotions and Distribution

Payola – Also known as pay for play, this now illegal practice is where PDs, MDs, or individual announcers accept money or gifts in exchange for airplay.

Plugola – In this illegal practice announcers give an on-air mention, or plug of an artist or business in exchange for money, services, or product.

Program Director (PD) – A managing employee of a radio station responsible for programming content for broadcast and daily operation of the station.

Promotions – The method by which information about the product being offered is communicated to the customer including public relations, advertising, sales promotions, and other tools to persuade customers to purchase the product offered. A promotional plan can have a wide range of objectives, including sales increases, new product acceptance, creation of brand, positioning, or creation of a corporate image.

Public Relations (PR) – a deliberate, planned, and sustained effort to manage the flow of information between a business or organization and its public. PR aims to establish and maintain a mutual understanding of an organization or product and seeks to gain positive exposure in their key market.

Publicity – This is the deliberate attempt to manage the public's perception of a subject or product. From a marketing perspective, publicity is one component of promotion.

Re-service – When you re-service you send the materials again.

Rotation – This is the frequency of which a song is scheduled for airplay. A song will typically fall into the category of light rotation, medium rotation, or heavy rotation. The heavier the rotation, the greater the spins.

Service – To service is to provide a single or project to a media outlet.

Shelf Life – The length of time a product may be stored without becoming unsuitable for use or consumption.

Spins – This is how many times a song has played during a given period of time.

SWAG – (Stuff We All Get) This is a term to describe bulk promotional items. For example, your CD would not count as SWAG, but pens you hand out or church fans with your image or t-shirts are considered SWAG. They are items individuals get to have at no expense to them.

Third Party Promoter – This is a individual or business working as a representative of the radio station who handles any rotation or music inquiries from a record label. A third party, not an in-house employee of the station, helps to minimize payola between labels and station personnel. Many, however, view this practice as a form of legal payola.

Tracking – This is the process of learning the status of a song. During the tracking process an artist or label rep will contact the program or music director regularly to continue to build relationship as well as learn the add status, rotation, and upcoming promotional opportunities.

Units – This is a term to count each CD project. The term unit is usually followed by a more descriptive term like "units sold" or "units manufactured."